The COMPANIONS *in* Christ®

Network

www.companionsinchrist.org

So much more!

Companions in Christ is *so much more* than printed resources.
It offers an ongoing LEADERSHIP NETWORK that provides:
- Opportunities to connect with other small groups who are also journeying through the *Companions in Christ* series
- Insights and testimonies from other *Companions in Christ* participants
- An online discussion room where you can share or gather information
- Training opportunities that develop and deepen the leadership skills used in formational groups
- Helpful leadership tips and articles as well as updated lists of supplemental resources
- A staff available to consult with you to meet the needs of your small group

Just complete this card and drop it in the mail, and you can enjoy the many benefits available through the *Companions in Christ* NETWORK!

Name: _____

Address: _____

City/State/Zip: _____

Church: _____

Email:_____ Phone: _____

WOBPB

COMPANIONS *in* Christ®
The Way of Blessedness

Please include your return address:

_____

_____

_____

BUSINESS REPLY MAIL

FIRST-CLASS MAIL PERMIT NO. 1540 NASHVILLE TN

POSTAGE WILL BE PAID BY ADDRESSEE

UPPER ROOM MINISTRIES
PO BOX 340012
NASHVILLE TN 37203-9540

COMPANIONS in Christ

The Way of Blessedness

PARTICIPANT'S BOOK

Marjorie J. Thompson and Stephen D. Bryant

UPPER ROOM BOOKS®
NASHVILLE

Cover design: Bruce Gore

Design and implementation: Lori Putnam

Cover art: Carter Bock

Cover art rendering: Marjorie J. Thompson

Interior icon development: Michael C. McGuire, settingPace

Second printing: 2004

Library of Congress Cataloging-in-Publication

Thompson, Marjorie J., 1953–
        Companions in Christ: the way of blessedness participant's book/ [Marjorie J. Thompson and Stephen D. Bryant].
                p. cm.
Includes bibliographical references.
        ISBN 0-8358-0992-7
        1. Christian life—Biblical teaching 2. Beatitudes—Study and teaching. 3. Small groups—Religious aspects—Christianity—Study and teaching. 4. Church group work. I. Bryant, Stephen D. II. Title.
BV4501.3.T473 2003
241.5'3—dc21   2003005792

Printed in the United States of America

For more information on *Companions in Christ*
call 800-972-0433 or visit www.companionsinchrist.org

Contents

Acknowledgments

The original twenty-eight week *Companions in Christ* resource grew from the seeds of a vision long held by Stephen D. Bryant, editor and publisher of Upper Room Ministries, and was given shape by Marjorie J. Thompson, director of the Pathways Center of Upper Room Ministries and spiritual director to the *Companions in Christ* Network. The vision, which has now expanded into the Companions in Christ series, was realized through the efforts of many people over many years. The original advisors, consultants, authors, editors, and test churches are acknowledged in the foundational twenty-eight week resource, as well as in the second title of the series, *Companions in Christ: The Way of Forgiveness*. We continue to owe an immense debt of gratitude to each person and congregation there named.

Companions in Christ: The Way of Blessedness is the third title in a series of shorter small-group resources that build on the foundation of *Companions in Christ*. The progression for the nine-week journey of *The Way of Blessedness* and the writing of the weekly articles in the Participant's Book are the primary work of Marjorie Thompson. The daily exercises in the Participant's Book and the deeper explorations in the Leader's Guide are the primary work of Stephen Bryant. A staff advisory team comprised of Lynne Deming, Cindy Helms, Tony Peterson, and Marjorie Thompson contributed to the completion of the

Acknowledgments

Leader's Guide. Mary Lou Redding served as a consultant and contributor of several ideas that influenced the final content of the Participant's Book. In addition, several Companions trainers offered valuable insight and guidance for developing *The Way of Blessedness*. This group included John Anderson, Ron Lagerstrom, Larry Peacock, Deborah Suess, Wynn McGregor, and Carole Cotton Winn.

The BEATITUDES

Blessed are the poor in spirit, for theirs is the kingdom of heaven.

Blessed are those who mourn, for they will be comforted.

Blessed are the meek, for they will inherit the earth.

*Blessed are those who hunger and thirst for righteousness,
for they will be filled.*

Blessed are the merciful, for they will receive mercy.

Blessed are the pure in heart, for they will see God.

*Blessed are the peacemakers, for they will be called
children of God.*

*Blessed are those who are persecuted for righteousness' sake,
for theirs is the kingdom of heaven.*

—From Jesus' Sermon on the Mount, Matthew 5:3-10

Introduction

*W*elcome to *Companions in Christ: The Way of Blessedness*, a small-group resource that explores Jesus' first teachings from the Sermon on the Mount commonly referred to as the Beatitudes. These teachings hold within them the key to realizing God's joy-filled intent for us—to live the soul-deep gladness and satisfaction of our faith. The path to which Christ calls us is certainly challenging. His teachings may first strike us as strange or confusing. But as we move forward on this journey, we trust you will discover for yourself and as a group how the way of blessedness calls us into the very life of God's kingdom.

In response to small groups who want to continue their exploration of spiritual practices that began with the original twenty-eight-week *Companions in Christ* resource, The Upper Room is developing the Companions in Christ series. *The Way of Forgiveness,* the second title in the series, offers an eight-week journey through the forgiven and forgiving life, keeping God's grace always before our eyes. *The Way of Blessedness* is the third title in the series.

Each resource in the Companions series expands the foundational content of the twenty-eight-week resource and uses the same basic format. In *Companions in Christ,* the foundational resource, we explored the Christian spiritual life under five headings: Journey, Scripture,

Prayer, Call, and Spiritual Guidance. Each supplementary volume will explore in greater depth some aspect of one of these five areas of spiritual life and practice.

The Way of Blessedness falls under the general heading of Scripture. The eight Beatitudes, found in Matthew 5:3-10, open Jesus' Sermon on the Mount (Matthew 5–7). Each statement is concise and direct, yet layered with profound wisdom. To explore the depth of these words, we will engage the Bible with mind and heart by drawing on classic practices of scriptural meditation and prayer. It is important to understand that this resource is not a Bible study in any traditional sense. It represents a formational approach to scripture more than an informational approach. Our interest lies in exploring the Beatitudes as a pathway of spiritual formation, discovering how the blessed life helps shape us into the fullness of the image of Christ.

Like the foundational program, *Companions in Christ*, this resource will help you deepen essential practices of the Christian life. It focuses on your daily experience of God and your growing capacity to respond to grace with gratitude, trust, love, and self-offering. Because this exploration takes place in the midst of a small group, you can expect increasingly to realize the blessings of mutual support, encouragement, guidance, and accountability in Christian community. Your growth in faith and maturation in spirit will benefit your congregation as well.

About the Resource and Process

Like all units of Companions in Christ, *The Way of Blessedness* has two primary components: individual reading and daily exercises throughout the week with this Participant's Book and a weekly two-hour meeting based on directions in the Leader's Guide.

Each weekly chapter in the Participant's Book introduces new material and provides five daily exercises to help you reflect on your life in light of the chapter content. After the Preparatory Meeting of your group, you will begin a weekly cycle as follows: On day 1 you will be asked to read the chapter; on days 2–6 you will complete each of the five daily exercises (found at the end of each chapter); on day 7 you will meet with your group.

The daily exercises aim to help you move from information (knowledge about) to experience (knowledge of). An important part of this process is keeping a personal notebook or journal where you record reflections, prayers, and questions for later review and for reference at the weekly group meeting. The time commitment for one daily exercise is approximately thirty minutes.

Weekly meetings include time for sharing reflections on the exercises of the past week and for moving deeper into the content of the chapter through various learning and prayer experiences. Meetings begin and end with simple worship times. You will need to bring your Participant's Book, your Bible, and your personal notebook or journal to each weekly group meeting. An annotated resource list on pages 105–111 describes Upper Room book titles related to the weekly themes.

The Companions in Christ Network

An additional dimension of resources in the Companions in Christ series is the Network. While you and your group are experiencing Companions, groups in other congregations will also be meeting. The Network provides opportunities for you to share your experiences with other groups and to link in a variety of meaningful ways. The Preparatory Meeting includes an invitation to link with another group through shared prayer, greetings, or small gifts. Connecting in these ways will enrich your group's experience and the experience of those to whom you reach out, helping develop the awareness of the wider reality of our companionship in the body of Christ across geographic and denominational lines.

The Network also provides a place to share conversation and information. The Companions' Web site, www.companionsinchrist.org, includes a discussion room where you can offer insights, voice questions, and respond to others in an ongoing process of shared learning. The site lists other Companions groups that are journeying

through each of the resources in the series and their geographical locations so that you can make contact as you feel led.

Your Personal Notebook or Journal

Keeping a journal or personal notebook (commonly called journaling) will be one of the most important dimensions of your personal experience with *Companions in Christ: The Way of Blessedness.* The Participant's Book gives you daily spiritual exercises each week. More often than not, you will be asked to note your thoughts, reflections, questions, feelings, or prayers in relation to the exercise.

You may find that this kind of personal writing quickly becomes second nature despite your inexperience. Your thoughts may start to pour out of you, giving expression to an inner life that has never been released. If, on the other hand, you find the writing difficult or cumbersome, give yourself permission to try it in a new way. Because a journal is "for your eyes only," you may choose any style that suits you. You need not worry about making your words sound beautiful or about writing with good grammar and spelling. You don't even need to write complete sentences. Jotting down key ideas, insights, or musings in a few words or phrases works just fine. You might doodle while you think or sketch an image that comes to you. Make journaling fun and relaxed. No one will see what you write, and you have complete freedom to share with the group only what you choose of your reflections.

Keeping a journal or personal notebook as you move through *The Way of Blessedness* is important for two reasons. First, the process of writing down thoughts clarifies them for us. They become more specific and concrete. Sometimes we really do not know what we think until we see our thoughts on paper; often the process of writing itself generates new creative insight. Second, this personal record captures our inward experience over time. Journaling helps us track changes in our thinking and growth of insight. Memories are notoriously fragile and fleeting in this regard. Specific feelings or creative connections we may have had two weeks ago or even three days ago, are hard to recall without a written record. Even though your journal cannot capture all that goes through your mind in a single reflection period, it will serve as a reminder. You will draw on these reminders during small-group meetings each week.

Begin by purchasing a book for this purpose. It can be as simple as a spiral-bound notebook or as fancy as a clothbound blank book. Some people prefer lined paper and some unlined. You will want, at minimum, something more permanent than a ring binder or paper pad. Upper Room Books has made available a Companions in Christ *Journal* that you may purchase if you wish.

When you begin the daily exercises, have your journal and pen or pencil at hand. You need not wait until you have finished reading and thinking an exercise through completely. Learn to stop and write as you go. Think on paper. Feel free to write anything that comes to you, even if it seems to be "off the topic." It may turn out to be more relevant or useful than you first believed. If the process seems clumsy at first, keep an open mind. Like any spiritual practice, it grows easier over time, and its value becomes more apparent.

Here is how your weekly practice of journaling is shaped. On the first day after your group meeting, read the new chapter. Jot down your responses to the reading: "aha" moments, questions, points of disagreement, images, or any other reflections you wish to record. You may prefer to note these in the margins of the Participant's Book. Over the next five days, you will do the exercises for the week, recording responses as they are invited. On the day of the group meeting, it will help to review what you have written through the week, perhaps marking portions you would like to share in the group. Bring your journal with you to meetings so that you can refer to it directly or refresh your memory about significant moments you want to paraphrase during discussion times. With time, you may find that journaling helps you to think out your own pattern of living and that you will be able to see more clearly how God is at work in your life.

Your Group Meeting

The weekly meeting is divided into four segments. First you will gather for a brief time of worship and prayer, which allows you to set aside the many concerns of the day and center on God's presence and guidance as you begin the group session.

The second section of the meeting is called "Sharing Insights." During this time the group leader will invite you to talk about your experiences with the daily exercises. The group leader will participate as a member and share his or her responses as well. Generally each member will briefly share thoughts and insights related to specific exercises. This sharing helps the group members learn and practice what it means to listen deeply. You are a community of persons seeking to listen to God and to one another so that you can live more faithfully as disciples of Christ. The group provides a supportive space to explore your listening, your spiritual practices, and your attempts to employ those practices in daily life.

The group does not function as a traditional support group where people are sometimes quick to offer advice or comment on one another's experiences. In *Companions* groups, members try to honor one another's experiences through prayerful attentiveness, affirmation, and respectful clarifying questions. The "Sharing Insights" part of the meeting is less meaningful when persons interrupt and comment on what is being said or try to "fix" what they see as a problem (called "cross talk"). Group members are invited to trust the Holy Spirit's guidance and help one another listen to that guidance.

The "Sharing Insights" time presents a unique opportunity to learn how God works differently in each life. Our journeys, while varied, enrich others' experiences. Other people's faith stories allow us to see anew how God's activity touches or addresses our lives in unexpected ways. The group will need to establish some ground rules to facilitate this sharing. Participants need clearly to agree that each person will speak only about his or her own beliefs, feelings, and responses and that all group members have permission to share only what and when they are ready to share. Above all, the group needs to maintain confidentiality so that what is shared in the group stays in the group.

The group leader participates in this sharing and aids the process by listening and summarizing key insights that have surfaced. The leader will close this part of the meeting by calling attention to any patterns or themes that seem to have emerged from the group sharing. These patterns may point to a word God is offering to the group.

The third segment of the group meeting is called "Deeper Explorations." This part of the meeting gives the group an opportunity to explore a deeper dimension of the beatitude for the week, to practice a spiritual discipline that is related to it, or to explore implications for one's life and church.

As it began, the group meeting ends with a brief time of worship when members may lift to God the needs and concerns that emerge from the experience of the meeting itself.

Invitation to the Journey

The weeks given to *The Way of Blessedness* offer you a unique opportunity to focus on your relationship with Jesus Christ and to grow in response to God's presence and guidance. Other members of your small group, truly your companions on the journey, will encourage your searching and learning as you encourage theirs.

In many respects, you will find that the Beatitudes draw you into a profound appreciation for our common Christian vocation. While the direct focus is scripture and the methods of exploration are scripturally based spiritual practices, the content of these teachings calls us to live in and under the reign of God. In the Beatitudes, Christ names the life he calls us to live. Through them he describes his vision of God's kingdom among us.

The life Jesus calls us to live is nothing short of complete conversion—a transformation of mind, heart, and action that reveals ever more fully the beauty and wholeness of his own spirit in us. This is what it means to be conformed to the image of Christ, the goal of spiritual formation in the Christian tradition. It is a goal we can conceive of only when we embrace God's grace. Yet that grace is

*God has nothing less
to give than
everything….
Of course it is too big
for us. But we are all
the same made for that
which is too big for us.*
    —Simon Tugwell

already available to us in Christ and is continually extended to us through the gift of the Holy Spirit. We open ourselves to grace most readily through prayer, faith, love for the deep truths of scripture, a willingness to be guided by the Spirit, and by offering ourselves in God's service.

So we invite you now to open yourself inwardly to the grace God desires to pour out upon you as you explore the spiritual riches of the blessed life. Remember that you can claim boldly from God the gifts you need to approach this topic. The life of the Spirit opens us to a true joy and happiness given to those who make a habit of following Jesus. May the grace of the Holy Spirit guide your footsteps as you follow him alongside your companions and sustain your journey into God's reign.

Exploring the Blessed Life

I have said these things to you so that my joy may be in you, and that your joy may be complete" (John 15:11). "I came that they may have life, and have it abundantly" (John 10:10). Abundant life! Complete joy! These are the gifts Jesus wants to give his followers of every generation. They are the highest gifts God can give to us. Are they not what our hearts most deeply crave?

We long for true joy, for deep contentment, for a full sense of blessedness in our lives. The world tries to give us answers by fulfilling our superficial desires and ego drives. Our culture thrives on consumer products promoted as a source of happiness: ample food, fashionable clothes, financial security. All sorts of business models, management tools, mental relaxation techniques, and physical conditioning will supposedly give us a competitive edge in life, thereby enhancing our sense of personal power and satisfaction. But the world's answers to our longing for deep joy do not finally fulfill us. They can sometimes leave us trapped in addictive cravings or simply feeling empty and lost. The world cannot give what only God can give.

Jesus, God's love made visible in human form, came with the joyful mission of helping us recover the things that make for deep happiness and satisfaction in life. He knew and embodied the secret of

true joy and delighted in sharing it with any who would listen. According to the Gospel of Matthew, Jesus shared many of his choicest spiritual pearls in a sermon preached early in his ministry. The full Sermon on the Mount spans three entire chapters in Matthew (5–7), but it begins with eight brief and pointed statements that Christians call the Beatitudes. The resource you hold in your hand, *The Way of Blessedness*, explores these eight teachings.

The Beatitudes

Beatitude is a rather quaint term, seldom used in common English speech. We find related words in a few familiar phrases such as "a beatific smile," in which beatific denotes something of the heavenly. Basically beatitude means "a state of blessedness or happiness," for biblical language makes the words *blessed* and *happy* virtually interchangeable.

> *Beatitude means "having everything you want," according to St. Augustine's definition…"and wanting nothing wrongly."*
> —Simon Tugwell

Yet, as we have already suggested, the kind of happiness Jesus points to in these teachings is far more profound than what we often think of as happiness. It moves beyond the superficial contentment that flits in and out in our lives, dependent on whether life is "going our way" and we are receiving complimentary attention. What Jesus means by happiness goes below the bubbling surface of life to the deep currents that run strong and steady beneath surface turbulence. Such happiness forms the bedrock joy in God that Jesus came to give us in the midst of all circumstances. It is the happiness of those who know and live in the reign of God.

The reign of God, or "kingdom of heaven" as Matthew's Gospel calls it, is central to everything that Jesus was and taught. Walter Wink notes with stunning insight that every word and deed of Jesus is like a hologram, "that marvelous laser photography in which the entire photographic image is preserved in any fragment of the negative."[1] Jesus came to reveal the nature of God's gracious rule and to show us what it looks like for a human being to live in the perfect freedom of a love governed by God's will. Jesus shows us a kingdom pattern of living and makes it possible for us to enter this divine realm of life by following the pattern he himself embodied. When we follow, we become his disciples.

We might think of the Beatitudes as a blueprint of kingdom life. If the Sermon on the Mount is core to Jesus' teaching ministry, the Beatitudes are the core of the core. In these few concise statements, Jesus paints a portrait of the citizen of the kingdom of God. Like a master Chinese calligrapher he paints in simple, bold strokes, each of which holds a world of meaning in itself yet maintains an integral connection with every other stroke to form the whole picture. The Beatitudes stand in the midst of the Gospel like a faceted gemstone, glinting and hinting at incredible depths of beauty. If we comprehend the reach of these words, we have grasped the essential teachings of Christ. To the extent that we live them, we become citizens of the kingdom, as was Jesus, and heirs with him of its privileges and responsibilities.

So the Beatitudes offer a "rule of life" for those who would be part of the new community called the kingdom of God. A rule of life is simply a way of life, a pattern of commitments we deliberately adopt to help us grow spiritually. Combining particular practices with the cultivation of certain attitudes or dispositions generally forms the pattern. Practices might include prayer, scriptural meditation, worship, fasting, and acts of service. Dispositions might include patience, kindness, gentleness, gratitude, and joy. Our practices and dispositions are mutually supportive, each reinforcing the other.

The Beatitudes speak primarily to dispositions of the soul, inward postures toward God, other people, ourselves, and the created order. They direct us to attitudes of mind and habits of heart that result in our actual way of being in the world. God's concern with what lies in our hearts makes the shaping of our inner perception and character crucial. Our words and deeds emerge from the dispositions of our souls. The Beatitudes point us, then, toward a "rule" of the inner life, helping us recognize and cultivate the dispositions that best suit us for the reign of God while drawing us into its realm.

The Reign of God

Perhaps it would be helpful to say more about this "kingdom of heaven" that is so utterly central to God's dream for humanity and therefore to Jesus' life and ministry. Jesus embodied and called into being around himself a new society that served as an expression of God's reign. This new society contradicted much of what was thought at the time to be essential to human community.

The culture of Jesus' day was full of hierarchical relationships. Wealthy landowners frequently cheated common laborers out of their meager wages because laborers had no power to prevent the master's unjust schemes. Households employed various kinds of servants and slaves, although Jewish slaves could not be forced to do some of the more menial tasks assigned to Gentile slaves, such as the degrading task of washing others' feet. Men exerted power over women, who were commonly viewed as property. Children held little value, although boys were allowed to go to school. Laws of ritual purity meant that people with greater means had higher religious status; the poor, for example, could not afford to keep two sets of utensils for a "kosher" kitchen. An identifiable group of social outcasts labeled "sinners" included tax collectors, adulterers, prostitutes, extortioners, idolaters, murderers, Samaritans, and Gentiles (that is, anyone outside the holiness code of Israel as interpreted by the religious leaders of that time). And over the whole hierarchy within Jewish culture lay the oppressive domination of the Roman occupation with its own hierarchical rules.[2]

Ancient Palestine based its social structures on distinctions of power and domination. In this respect Jesus' world did not differ much from ours. We still live under systems of domination, assuming that control by the powerful and wealthy is a fact of life. We have our own ways of creating hierarchies of influence, our own ways of valuing certain kinds of people over others based on education, income, name recognition, or success—if not on race, ethnicity, gender, or age.

Such distinctions didn't interest Jesus. His interest lay in the heart and soul of all human beings, whatever their role or place in society.

He sat at the tables of influential leaders and ate with sinners with equal composure and purpose. He healed the Roman centurion's servant just as he made whole the poorest Jewish peasant. He taught with transforming power the respected Pharisee Nicodemus and the despised tax collector Zacchaeus.

The kingdom Jesus proclaimed would have borne no similarity to any kingdom his listeners had known. This kingdom did not function based on dominating power or the self-interest of a ruling elite. Indeed, the chief ruler of this realm, God, was unlike any oriental potentate or Roman emperor with whom they were familiar. God, Jesus says, is like a father who waits patiently for the return of a son who has disgraced himself and his family (Luke 15:11-32). Or God is like the host who will send out his servant to collect the poor, the crippled, the blind, and the lame to fill up a banquet when the "proper" guests are too busy with their own agendas to come (Luke 14:5-24). God, like a landowner who pays the last hired workers of the day the same amount as those who have worked all day (Matt. 20:1-16), displays a depth of compassion and an uncommon concern for the least and last, an outlandish generosity.

Jesus portrays the realm of God in terms that do not support social hierarchy. He uses earthy, humble images to describe God's reign: yeast that a woman takes and mixes into dough until all is leavened (Matt. 13:33); a tiny mustard seed that somehow grows from a shrub into a large tree under which creatures may take refuge (Matt. 13:31-32). The reign of God rises up from below, rather than being imposed from above, emerging from the hidden mystery of divine spirit at work in the heart of creation. The humble and simple reign of God equalizes people—women and men, children and adults, servants and masters. It embraces the whole creation.

Not surprisingly, those who felt liberated by this equalizing message to stand tall, those who heard it as good news, were Jesus' primary audience. Matthew portrays those who came to listen to the Sermon on the Mount as "great crowds...from Galilee, the Decapolis, Jerusalem, Judea, and from beyond the Jordan" (4:25). Indeed, Jesus' fame spread rapidly as he preached the "good news of the kingdom"

There was a radical social and political edge to [Jesus'] message and activity. He challenged the social order of his day and indicted the elites who dominated it.

—Marcus J. Borg

and cured all manner of diseases. His healing acts and proclamation of God's reign went hand in hand, for healing was a visible expression of God's merciful presence and rule. In his own person, Jesus' proclamation was fulfilled: "The kingdom of heaven has come near" (Matt. 4:17). As an embodiment of God's reign, Jesus made himself available to the poor, the sick, the outcast, and the oppressed—those believed by upright Jewish citizens to be marked by God's displeasure. As emissary of God's kingdom "come near," Jesus habitually associated with sinners, touched the "unclean," talked with women in public, broke the rigid laws that dictated social convention. These associations got people's attention: wondering, yearning attention from the commoners and irritated suspicion from the powerful.

Here, among crowds of ordinary people who suffered from illnesses, who toiled hard for small wages, who were routinely disregarded and devalued, Jesus began his sermon. He was ready to share the secret of a truly joyful and blessed life, a life given over in love to God's reign. To eyes and ears trained by a world with vastly different values and objectives, his did not always sound like a blessed way. Just as his own hearers often failed to grasp Jesus' meaning, we may struggle to find the meaning of his wisdom for our time. Yet if we, like those in the crowd, can come ready to listen and willing to imagine a realm far better than we know, we will discover in Jesus' way of life the "pearl of great value" that our souls desire above all else.

Perhaps along the way we will be ready to consider how we can cultivate Beatitude dispositions that become part of our "rule of life" or regular way of life. We can practice postures of humility, gentleness, generosity, and joy just as surely as we can practice piano scales or basketball shots. As we offer to God an integrated pattern of intention and commitment for maturing in spirit, we can trust the Holy Spirit gradually to transform us into genuine citizens of the new society, the realm of God—not just for the future consummation of that kingdom but also here and now as we live out our discipleship in a world desperate for practical spiritual wisdom.

Deep inside the spiritual wisdom of the Beatitudes lies a paradox that runs through the heart of the gospel: The power within and behind the entire universe does not assert itself as raw power; it is, rather, revealed in self-effacing humility and love. Jesus shows us the transforming power of the self-emptying love of God. Although in the "form of God," he "did not count equality with God a thing to be grasped, but emptied himself, taking the form of a servant" (Phil. 2:6-7, RSV).

It is the nature of love to go out of itself to the other. The Christian spiritual life means participating with Christ in the self-emptying born of love. Each beatitude represents a way of participating in the self-emptying love of Christ. And the Christian spiritual life begins with poverty of spirit. The most difficult to interpret well, this beatitude nonetheless grounds all the rest. Without poverty of spirit there is no access to the reign of God. Upon its foundation, all the beatitudes build in an integrated sequence like "steps on the stairway into the kingdom."[3]

Are you ready to be challenged and blessed by Jesus' greatest teachings? If so, enter this journey through the Beatitudes with your companions. There is much of this world to lose, but the whole kingdom of heaven is ours to gain.

DAILY EXERCISES

This week's reading reminds us of the great love and good will God extends to us and introduces us to the blessed life into which God invites us. Read Week One, "Exploring the Blessed Life," before moving into the daily exercises. As you begin to reflect on the exercises below, have your journal available to record your thoughts, reflections, and questions. These recorded reflections will help you recall your daily experiences as you prepare to share your insights in the weekly group meeting. In preparation for each exercise, take a moment to clear your mind of distractions. When your mind and soul find rest, you will be open to the fullness each daily exercise has for you.

EXERCISE 1 BLESSED TO BE A BLESSING

Read Genesis 12:1-3. God blessed Abram and Sarai so that they would "be a blessing" to "all the families of the earth." Take a few moments to count your blessings. List the names of people who, like Abram and Sarai, have been a means of blessing in your life. Beside each name, write out the nature of the blessing you received.

Read back over your memories and reflect on what God has been up to in your life. For what purpose has God been blessing you? In what sense would you describe your life as blessed to "be a blessing"? Write out your thoughts.

EXERCISE 2 BLESSED WITH PRESENCE AND PURPOSE

Read Matthew 3:13-17. Through John's ministry, Jesus experienced the blessing of God's presence and promise in a memorable way: confirmation of his identity and purpose in life. Name two or three holy moments or special experiences through which God blessed you with a sense of divine presence or purpose. What gift did you receive from each of those experiences?

EXERCISE 3 HEARING ANEW THE CALL OF CHRIST

Read Matthew 4:18-22. Jesus called the disciples in the midst of their everyday life and work. When and where do you first remember hearing Christ calling you to follow? Draw a rough time line of your life (early, middle, and recent years) and mark periods when Christ's call seemed to be coming through to you. Make some notes on what you heard each time and your response.

Ponder how you are hearing Christ's call at this time in your life. Complete this line for yourself: "Follow me, and I will make you _____." Write out your thoughts on Christ's call and promise in your life now.

EXERCISE 4 BEING CLEAR ABOUT WHAT JESUS BLESSES

Read Matthew 5:1-10. Note in your journal the forms of blessedness that most attract you. What blessing do you long to receive and grow in? Also note the blessings that give you pause. What in these blessings do you fear, resist, or question? In which of these areas do you also long to grow?

Draw a line down the middle of a page in your journal. Title one side "What the World Blesses" and the other side "What God Blesses." Jot down words and phrases that come to mind in the first column, those things Jesus does not bless but that our culture blesses instead. Then, remembering and expanding on what Jesus calls blessed, jot down words and phrases that come to mind in the second column.

Reflect on your lists. Which column of words and phrases seems more representative of the path you are on? Take note of where you find yourself wanting to go both directions at once. Look at yourself with honest compassion now. Where would Jesus celebrate what he already sees in you? Where do you hear Jesus calling forth something new in you? Pray as the Spirit leads you. Note any insights in your journal.

EXERCISE 5 CELEBRATING THE KINGDOM'S NEARNESS

Read Matthew 4:17. Jesus' first proclamation of the kingdom represents the thrust of his entire ministry—his teachings and his actions. How would you state or express the message in your own words? What image would show what the nearness of God's kingdom means to you? Consider drawing that image in your journal.

Reflect on the beatitudes (Matthew 5:3-10 or page 7 of this Participant's Book) as clues to where Jesus saw and celebrated the kingdom of heaven's coming near. When or where did the kingdom "come near" to you in the past week? Review your week day by day in your mind and allow the Spirit to open your heart to the nearness of God's kingdom. Jot down each memory. Select one and explore more fully what you saw and felt.

Give thanks in prayer for the nearness of God's kingdom as you are experiencing it.

Remember to review the insights recorded in your notebook or journal for the week in preparation for the group meeting.

Week 2
Embracing Our Spiritual Poverty

"Blessed are the poor in spirit,
for theirs is the kingdom of heaven."

M any years ago I recall my mother railing against this beatitude. It made no sense to her. Why, she exclaimed, would Jesus commend people who are "lacking in spirit"? Why, indeed? Flora Wuellner calls "poor in spirit" a most unfortunate translation, evoking for many people an image of "spiritless, disempowered, washed-out victims."[1] What did Jesus mean by "poor in spirit"? This beatitude may be the most difficult to interpret, and some understandings are less helpful than others.

For example, some suggest that this beatitude refers to our moral and spiritual impoverishment. We are often "rich in things and poor in soul." In our nose-length focus on the goods of this world we risk missing the kingdom's goal. As one spiritual writer notes, "A full hand helps a [person] to forget an empty heart."[2] This understanding of spiritual poverty refers primarily to the weakness of human sin in all its unhappy forms.

Our moral and spiritual bankruptcy represents a genuine truth about the human condition and could certainly be viewed as a form of spiritual poverty. But Jesus surely would not have called such a state blessed nor presented it as an entry point into the kingdom of God. What other interpretations of this beatitude exist?

To some, being poor in spirit means being free from covetousness and love of money. This understanding closely links poverty of

spirit with simplicity of life and a gratitude that does not depend on the "security" of wealth. Others believe we can cultivate an inward spirit of poverty even in the midst of material abundance, since the inner life does not always correspond directly to outward circumstances. These perspectives, while helpful, do not take us far enough.

Clarence Jordan, the earthy Baptist preacher and scholar who wrote the "Cotton Patch Version" of the New Testament, observes that "it is neither wealth nor poverty that keeps people out of the kingdom—it is pride."[3] There is much truth in his words, yet pride is not the only sin barring entry into God's realm. Self-loathing and despair born of shame are equally effective barriers to love. Knowing our sins of pride and self-degradation keeps us mindful of our need for God's cleansing and healing grace.

But even if we were not sinners at all, we would depend utterly on God for our life and happiness. Our poverty before God in this sense is an essential key to being truly human. Perhaps we can now begin to see why Jesus begins the Beatitudes with the words, "Blessed are the poor in spirit." In a profound sense, poverty of spirit is the basis for every beatitude that follows, the critical foundation for citizenship in God's realm.

The Holy Spirit is called the Giver of Gifts…but this cherishing action is only really felt by those who acknowledge their own deep poverty.

—Evelyn Underhill

Spiritual Poverty As Radical Dependence on God

A great Christian philosopher once remarked that every human being contains a God-shaped void that only God can fill. We are not complete in and of ourselves. "There is a radical resourcelessness in human life,"[4] spiritually speaking. We are not self-made. Our very identity and purpose is rooted in God, not ourselves. We find ourselves restless with doubt and dissatisfaction—finite physically, mentally, and emotionally. Our lives in this world are uncertain and insecure. They can be irreversibly changed or taken from us in a single moment, by accident, violence, natural catastrophe, or through a hidden weakness in our bodies. "Of all creatures we are the poorest and the most incomplete. Our needs are always beyond our capacities, and we only find ourselves when we lose ourselves."[5] It is hard to accept the provisional quality of human life. Yet without God at the center we cannot be what God has made us to be—truly human.

In this fundamental poverty, Jesus is our greatest teacher. As a human being he models for us complete dependence on God. He claims no power of his own, no word to teach, no wisdom to offer but that of his heavenly "Abba." "Very truly, I tell you, the Son can do nothing on his own, but only what he sees the Father doing" (John 5:19). Again and again Jesus points not to himself but to God: "I seek to do not my own will but the will of him who sent me," he tells his disciples in John's Gospel (5:30). "Why do you call me good? No one is good but God alone," he says to the rich man who asks how to inherit eternal life (Mark 10:18).

The depth of divine poverty and humility in Christ is perhaps best captured in the passage from Philippians mentioned in the Introduction: "Though he was in the form of God, [he] did not count equality with God a thing to be grasped, but emptied himself, taking the form of a servant" (2:6-7, RSV). Jesus shows us the true meaning of poverty of spirit: a mature, freely accepted dependence on God's gracious and powerful love, the source of all human empowerment. Indeed, the strength and transforming effect of Jesus' ministry come from a willing surrender of his will to God's.

> *Did not Jesus live in continual dependence on Someone else? Was not his very existence hidden in the mysterious will of the Father?*
> —Johannes Baptist Metz

Embracing Our Poverty

We are all poor in spirit in the sense of needing divine empowerment to become fully human. But we find it hard to own this poverty and to embrace it. Poverty of spirit threatens our worldly sense of personal value and our illusions of self-originating creativity. We would much prefer to be "rich in spirit," possessing wisdom, knowledge, and truth to pass on to others. Of course, at times we have wisdom and knowledge to pass on to others, but these truths are not wholly original to us. They come as gifts, filtered through our own and others' experiences or welling up as insights from a mysterious source beyond us. All that we are and have is a gift.

Our insufficiencies and limitations become clear to us in different

ways. Sometimes we simply feel overwhelmed by what life puts on our plate. "It never rains but it pours," we say ruefully when work and family responsibilities pile up all at once. Sometimes we truly believe we can't make it through the day or do what is expected of us in a single week. My husband and I recently had a year so filled with responsibilities for three aging parents and several household moves, along with two full-time jobs, that we could scarcely imagine how to get from one month to the next. Yet grace abounded for us through the faithful prayers of many friends and colleagues. During that time I learned a good deal about my own insufficiencies—in time, energy, clarity, patience, and sheer capacity to cope. Above all, I found myself coming empty to God over and over, offering my weakness in hope and trust, asking for the strength and grace needed for each day. Grace was given, sometimes with an abundance that took my breath away. Yet every day offered a new opportunity to embrace my essential dependence on God.

Poverty of spirit takes many forms. If you have ever discovered that you cannot do what God wants simply by depending on your own intelligence, skill, energy, or self-control, you have faced something of your own spiritual poverty. The writer Judy Cannato identified her hearing loss as a form of spiritual poverty that drew her into a profound listening to God. A single father, raising a mentally disabled child, came to realize how the limits of his own energy and wisdom became an occasion for his community of faith to exercise their ministry of caring support. Over the course of our lives, we all suffer different kinds of more visible impairment or diminished abilities. These can be opportunities to discover God's transformation of our poverty into rich experiences of grace, for ourselves and often for others. Cannato discovered that saying yes to her impoverished hearing with as much freedom and love as she could offer allowed her to experience a delightful paradox: "It is my hearing loss that is my greatest hearing aid."[6] Can we say yes in love and freedom to the particular chalice of limitation God offers to us? What paradoxes might we discover in our own poverty of spirit?

The individual guises of this poverty are the possibilities bestowed on us by God…. They are the chalice that God holds out to us.

—Johannes Baptist Metz

The Invitation

The question before us is this: Will we embrace our deep need for God? Will we accept the finite container of our lives as an opportunity for God's infilling grace? If we willingly open to the divine Mystery in humility and trust, we become like the child Jesus placed among his disciples when he said, "Unless you change and become like children, you will never enter the kingdom of heaven." Trusting dependence opens to us the realm of God's love, a realm where neither proud self-sufficiency nor despairing self-deprecation can abide. Here lies the source of all true blessedness and empowerment.

The joyful paradox of our spiritual poverty is that God's fullness can flow through our emptiness; in our weakness God's power can be revealed; in our insufficiency grace suffices. Richness of spirit belongs to God who gives generously according to our need and receptivity. We discover that depending fully on God's grace in no way diminishes us but strengthens the original goodness of the divine image in which we are created. So our spiritual poverty is our glory, for through it grace shines unobstructed, and God is glorified through the unique lens that each of us is created to be.

To know and live this deep, joyful truth places us directly in God's gracious reign. Jesus says in effect, "When you give up your illusions of control or helplessness and accept your need for God, all that God has opens to you." In embracing our need and accepting God's life-giving gifts, we enter the realm of God's guiding reign.

The call to holiness is the call to be free to be nothing, free to be poor so that God can use us for anything.

—Ed Farrell

DAILY EXERCISES

Read and reflect on Week Two, "Embracing Our Spiritual Poverty." As you move through the daily exercises, be open to discovering where in your life you are poor in spirit and where God may be calling you to empty yourself. Remember to take a few minutes to center yourself in preparation for the daily reflection.

EXERCISE 1   LISTENING TO JESUS

Read Matthew 4:23–5:3. Survey the scene and notice the different forms of poverty in the people who came to Jesus. Where do you see your own poverty? What need or desire brings you to Jesus and to this course?

Sit with Jesus' blessing for a while. Turn his words over in your mind. When Jesus saw the crowds in other places, the Gospel writers often tell us that "he had compassion for them" (Matt. 9:36; 14:14). So listen to Jesus' blessing here as coming from the heart of God's great compassion for the "poor" (Luke 6:20) and "the poor in spirit" (Matt. 5:3). Listen with your heart as well as your head.

Try writing this blessing in your own words, as many different ways as you like. Which way touches you? Which way would touch and encourage those to whom your heart goes out these days?

Spend a few moments in prayer. Assume a posture of utter receptivity to God, the fount of every blessing. Bring your need, especially the need with which you come to this study, before God with open hands. Record the essence of your prayer.

EXERCISE 2   LEARNING TO RELY ON GOD

Read Psalm 131. This psalm invites us to rest in God by coming before God "like a weaned child with its mother," in utter trust and humility. Let the psalm lead you into prayer in poverty of spirit, being entirely open and present to God.

Dwell on each line, repeating it prayerfully. Take time to assume the interior posture with God to which each verse invites you. Pray with the psalm in this way for several minutes.

Pause from time to time to speak directly with God. Tell God your preoccupations as they come to mind. Above all, maintain your gaze upon the One who holds you. Record your experience.

EXERCISE 3   BECOMING LIKE A CHILD

Read Mark 10:13-16. Call to mind the face of a child whom you know. Today as you have opportunities to observe or spend time with children, consider what you could learn from them about what it means to be poor in spirit and "receive the kingdom." What do you need to unlearn in order to "receive the kingdom of God as a little child"?

In a time of prayer, imagine yourself as one of the little children being brought to Jesus. Hear and respond to Jesus' invitation, "Let the little children come to me." Let Jesus take you "up in his arms," lay "his hands on" you, and bless you. Enjoy a time of letting yourself be loved just as you are.

Consider how you might extend this blessing to someone else. Who is this someone? Use this image as a way of praying for him or her. Write of your experience in your journal.

EXERCISE 4   BEING REAL WITH GOD

Read Luke 18:9-14. In this story, Jesus sharply contrasts the proud in spirit and the poor in spirit. Look for areas where you see both of these characters in yourself. For example, in what ways are you like the Pharisee, having your spiritual act together on the outside but inwardly lacking? In what ways are you like the tax collector, having made a mess of your life in anyone's judgment but knowing your need for God's help?

Write in your journal about where and how you see yourself in the story.

Join the tax collector in prayer. This prayer, along with the prayer of Bartimaeus in Mark 10:46-52, is the scriptural basis of the ancient Jesus Prayer: "Lord Jesus Christ, Son of God, have mercy on me, a sinner" or simply, "Lord, have mercy." Recite his words for several minutes and formulate for yourself what is called a "breath prayer." As you say, "God, be merciful to me, a sinner," exercise complete

freedom to customize this brief prayer as you please so as to address God with the holy name you prefer and to make your need specific (for example, "God, have mercy on me"; "Jesus, give me your peace"; "Master, show me the way"; "Savior, like a shepherd lead me"; or "Lord, make your presence known to me"). Keep the prayer brief and memorable. Sit with it now and practice being present to God just as you are for several minutes.

Write about your experience with your breath prayer.

EXERCISE 5   MAKING SPACE FOR GOD

Read Philippians 2:1-11. With this ancient hymn, the apostle Paul celebrates the remarkable paradox that Jesus, though rich in God, became poor in spirit in obedience to God.

Recall in your mind the life and spirit of Jesus. Of what do you see Jesus emptying himself in order to be God's servant "in human likeness" (v. 7)?

Of what do you need to be emptied in order to make room for the life Christ offers and invites you to share with him? Read the passage again; then prayerfully dwell on verses 6-8. Look into your heart for where and how you need to make space for God's great gift and call. Imagine the empowered life that could flow through you as you allow such space for God.

Write your insights in your journal.

Remember to review the insights recorded in your notebook or journal for the week in preparation for the group meeting.

Tears As Anguish, Tears As Gift

*"Blessed are those who mourn,
for they will be comforted."*

I wonder if Jesus ever lost a family member and knew what that felt like?" Ten-year-old Lindsey mused sadly three months after she lost her favorite aunt to breast cancer. Lindsey's Sunday school class had been memorizing the Beatitudes, and this one did not make sense to her. "I don't understand why Jesus says mourning is blessed," she declared. "And I don't feel comforted either."

Lindsey's observation brings into bold relief the seeming absurdity of this beatitude. Anyone who has ever experienced the long, aching emptiness of deep grief knows it is anything but blessed. What kind of comfort adequately assuages real grief? Yet Jesus' words challenge us to plumb them for meanings not readily apparent. Our Lord's teachings often address more than one level of meaning. What possibilities of blessing lie hidden within our mourning?

> *It is impossible for one to live without tears who considers things exactly as they are.*
> —Gregory of Nyssa

Tears of Grief

Our most common experience of mourning comes through losses by death. Indeed, the Hebrew and Greek words for "mourning" in scripture most often refer to the personal emotion or communal ritual of grief resulting from a person's death.

Intensely personal grief grips us upon the death of a loved one. Shock, numbness, and disbelief mark its early phase. After numbness

comes the permeating pain of irreversible loss. Tears seem endless, threatening to overwhelm us emotionally. Deep grief, like a bad dream from which we cannot awake, becomes all-encompassing and inescapable. It may involve a shattered sense of security, disorientation, extreme fatigue with sleeplessness, fear of abandonment, or bitterly shaken faith. Depression and despair are not uncommon. Even when expected, death generally frightens us. The passage between life and death is such a mystery.

With time the acute phase of grief diminishes, yet it continues to well up and overwhelm us periodically. I recall a friend's telling me, some months after his father's death, that grief would catch him unexpectedly: "It is like standing in the ocean facing the shore and having a huge wave come up and hit you from behind. You don't see it coming." A mere fragrance, sight, or strain of music can tumble us beneath the billows of grief again. Such mourning is a long agony, far from what we would consider any form of blessedness.

Experiences of Comfort

Yet despite such pain, people who grieve can often identify blessings directly related to their losses. One blessing frequently named is the support of family, friends, neighbors, and colleagues. Sometimes God places someone in our way, even a complete stranger, who offers a touch of grace. In times of crisis we learn to treasure the small, unspectacular gestures of care: a word, a hand, an expression in the eyes. One professor of theology used to dismiss as shallow the tradition of bringing casseroles to grieving families. But upon his wife's death, he discovered how meaningful and comforting that ritual was. The physical and emotional help of receiving prepared food at a time of physical depletion and mental preoccupation became a sign of God's hospitality and grace. He has developed a "casserole" theology.

Mourners quickly learn that the greatest comfort in a time of unspeakable loss is the simple presence of another human being. Well-intentioned Christians sometimes try to comfort with trite platitudes: "It must have been God's will," or "God just wanted your little girl to be an angel in heaven." Efforts to explain divine intent rarely help someone in grief. But blessing may arrive in a person who comes and weeps with you. Comfort comes through human solidarity in pain, making us feel less alone.

Another category of blessing named by those who grieve is the gift of new perspective. Loss can confront us abruptly with a different view of what matters most in life. Many who lost loved ones in the attacks of September 11, 2001, found themselves resetting their priorities. I recall listening to one woman on a radio report tell how her moneymaking goals seemed suddenly so meaningless. In the face of massive human loss she had undergone a radical inner shift. She now focused on strengthening her relationships of love, appreciating each day, and taking nothing for granted.

The death of someone dear can prompt healthy self-examination. Permanent absence in an important relationship often enables us to see ourselves more clearly. We may recognize self-centered life patterns or the real value of a trait in the deceased that used to "drive us crazy." Sometimes we mature in ways that could not have occurred had the loved one remained in our lives. Loss stretches, sobers, shapes, and strengthens us. The blessing comes in growth we often see only in hindsight.

A third arena of blessing in grief is the comfort of our faith. The Christian faith has much to say to us concerning life, death, and meaning. The promises extended to those with faith are distinctive and powerful: "Even though I walk through the darkest valley, I fear no evil; for you are with me"(Ps. 23:4). "I am the resurrection and the life. Those who believe in me, even though they die, will live" (John 11:25). "'And if I go and prepare a place for you, I will come again and will take you to myself, so that where I am, there you may be also'" (John 14:3). "The dead will be raised imperishable, and we will be changed" (1 Cor. 15:52).

But even before we receive the benefit of such promises, faith brings blessing in the time of loss. Facing the reality of death throws us onto the mercy and grace of God. It tears away the illusion of self-reliance, the presumption that we can control—for ourselves or for

It is grief that strips us to a genuine humility.
—Walter Wangerin

others—the time given us to live. Death presents a potential crisis of faith. We will either despair of God's reality and goodness or learn to trust God's greater unseen purpose. The end of life as we know it provides an opportunity for spiritual growth. We may accept or reject the opportunity, but even acceptance comes only with struggle.

Other kinds of loss in life share the dynamic of death. A divorce marks the death of a marriage relationship and can be as painful emotionally as physical death. The grief that comes from being unable to conceive or bear a child represents the loss of a potential and deeply desired relationship. We may mourn the loss of a job, especially if we have loved our work and felt we were using our best gifts in it. The loss of a job may also entail loss of self-esteem. If we grew up in a "dysfunctional family," perhaps we mourn the caring, nurturing family life we never had. We may mourn the loss of mental or physical abilities, grieving the death of parts of ourselves. We may mourn the loss of home and possessions through fire, natural disaster, or war. Refugees grieve for their homeland, a place of familiar life and community. All these forms of grief carry us to a deeper level of meaning in Jesus' words, "Blessed are those who mourn, for they will be comforted."

Tears of Contrition

In theological language, death is "the wages of sin" (Rom. 6:23). Sin describes every way we are alienated from God: our failure to see what God intends for human community; our fear of becoming what God made us to be; the effort to live out of our own desires and resources. Sin is our need to take control of things, using wit and grit to create the reality we want. Sin reflects our anxiety about self-worth and lack of courage to live up to our calling. Both in our offensive drive to remake the world and our defensive avoidance of responsibility, we can hurt others, ignore God, despoil the earth, and destroy the beauty of our own souls. Pride, fear, jealousy, and greed scar our relationships, from family life to international politics.

Spiritual death is human life exiled from God—no life at all for the long haul. As Jesus said, "Apart from me you can do nothing"

(John 15:5). We "live" cut off from the Source of life. Saint Augustine linked the beatitude on mourning with the gift of knowledge. Commenting on Augustine's insight, one contemporary writer observes, "To know the truth of our human predicament is to know it as something that can be met only with mourning."[1]

The idea of mourning our sins is deeply rooted in the biblical tradition. Penitential fasting and putting on sackcloth and ashes signaled the mourning of sin. King David mourned his adultery while his infant son born to Bathsheba struggled to live (see 2 Sam. 12:16-23). The king hoped his humility and contrition would prompt God to spare his son. After the child's death, the king stopped his penitential mourning, though he undoubtedly continued to mourn his son's death.

Some scholars believe that the author of Matthew's Gospel specifically had penitential mourning in mind in this beatitude. They point to a later passage in Matthew, where Jesus explains why his disciples did not fast as did those of John the Baptist: "The wedding guests cannot mourn as long as the bridegroom is with them, can they? The days will come when the bridegroom is taken away from them, and then they will fast" (9:15). Again in Matthew's Gospel, Jesus teaches that at the end of the age "all the tribes of the earth will mourn" at the sign of the Son of Man (24:30), clearly penitential mourning.

To mourn the sad state of our world and our complicity in it is a first step toward the blessedness Jesus offers. We cannot move beyond our sin until we have learned to mourn it. If we do not care deeply about the desperate needs and pains of this world, we will not find ourselves "in the way" of the Beatitudes.

Realism about the world is not a source of despair or cynicism for Christians. We simply join our Lord who mourned so deeply over our hard-hearted foolishness: "Jerusalem, Jerusalem, the city that kills the prophets....How often have I desired to gather your children together as a hen gathers her brood under her wings, and you were not willing!" (Matt. 23:37). The Gospels express Jesus' grief over human stubbornness, blindness, fear, and faithlessness at many points. His mourning focused on the destructive effects of sin and finally became

The suffering that our Lord pronounces blessed is the genuine suffering of an honest awareness of and involvement in the breakdown of our world, our society, ourselves. It is the mourning of the realist, the penitent.

—Simon Tugwell

embodied in his passion. The writer of Hebrews gives us a glimpse of the intensity of Jesus' grief: "In the days of his flesh, Jesus offered up prayers and supplications, with loud cries and tears" (5:7).

What do we mourn with cries and tears? What situations in this world or in our own lives do we grieve with genuine sorrow? To mourn with Christ our true condition does not mean that we despise or condemn our brokenness. Jesus does not despise or condemn us. Even the worst evils are human dignity and goodness gone terribly wrong. Indignation over sin tends to puff us up, but humility keeps us rooted in compassion.

Comfort for Mourning

Compassion literally means "to suffer with." When we experience our mourning as participation in the suffering of Christ, we begin to know the blessing of sorrow. In Christ all suffering, sin, and misery have been taken up and transfigured by God's love. Redemption means the transformation of every form of death into new life. And this new life is God's gift to us out of sheer, tender mercy. We can do nothing in our own power to redeem this world or ourselves. The remedy for the sorry truth of our plight is totally beyond us. "No amount of achievement can overcome death."[2] In the helplessness of mourning our sin, we discover again our poverty of spirit.

The inner connection between spiritual poverty and mourning is poignantly evident in the story of Dwight Vogel's Uncle Milton, a pastor. Milton and his wife, Grace, were celebrating their fortieth wedding anniversary with their son, daughter, and two grandchildren on a small showboat on Lake Pomona, Kansas, when a freak tornado capsized the boat. Grace, daughter Sandra, and granddaughter Melissa all drowned. In an instant, women from three generations of the family were suddenly gone. In the week that followed, someone said to Milton, "I don't know how you can go on." "There isn't any alternative," he replied. "All my ministry I've told others that God is good. God loves and cares. God's grace is sufficient for every need. Now I know there is nothing else on which we can rely."[3]

Knowing "nothing else on which we can rely" is the experience of being poor in spirit. In our deep mourning over the many forms of death and suffering in this life, we drink the dregs of our poverty. Yet at this point, blessing comes to life. Our empty, aching hearts— open to the indwelling grace of God—allow our weakness to become a vessel for God's power; mourning invites the fulfillment of the promises of scripture.

Comfort belongs to disciples who mourn. While we cannot change the fact of death, we can join Jesus' redeeming work in this world. Indeed, as disciples we are commanded to do so: "Love one another as I have loved you" (John 15:12). "Bear one another's burdens, and in this you will fulfill the law of Christ" (Gal. 6:2). Do you believe that "it is God who is at work in you, enabling you both to will and to work for [God's] good pleasure" (Phil. 2:13)? If so, you know that God's comfort comes through people of faith like yourself. Each of us can become an expression of the kingdom of heaven on earth, bearing God's compassionate heart to one another.

The fullness of the promise and the complete comfort of faith belong to God's future. We know that Christ has already gathered humanity into himself and made it whole by his loving sacrifice. We can trust that even now all things are made new in Christ. But hear this further promise of completion when the work begun in Christ will be fully manifest: In "a new heaven and a new earth" shown to the writer of Revelation, "Death will be no more; mourning and crying and pain will be no more" (21:1, 4). God will wipe away every tear from our eyes. What a vision of comfort in God's eternal realm!

It is only when our hearts break, that they break open: then the word of God can enter deeply, like a seed in a harrowed field.
—Deborah Smith Douglas

DAILY EXERCISES

This week's reading and exercises give you an opportunity to consider how you have experienced mourning in your own life, in the lives of those around you, in the world, and in the life of Christ. The reflections for this week may take you to tender places in your life. Recall Christ's words, "They will be comforted." Read Week Three, "Tears As Anguish, Tears As Gift," before beginning your daily exercises. Record your thoughts, questions and reflections in your journal. To prepare yourself for your daily time of reflection, sit quietly for a few minutes and invite God to be your guide and comforter.

EXERCISE 1   LISTENING TO JESUS

Read Matthew 5:4. As you turn Jesus' words over in your mind, identify a time of deep mourning in your life. In your journal, describe what it felt like and its effect on you. Also reflect on where you found real comfort. How does Jesus' blessing speak to you?

Clarence Jordan interprets "those who mourn" as those "deeply concerned" about the state of their lives and of the world. What deep concern do you bear within your heart, a concern so deep that you feel called to do something about it? Write about your concern.

Listen again to Jesus' blessing. How would you paraphrase the beatitude in your own words?

EXERCISE 2   PARTICIPATING IN GOD'S CONCERN

Read Isaiah 40:1-5. Through this passage, God calls Isaiah to comfort people who have been in mourning over their exile from home for a long time. Who are the people of our day whose misery you know and deeply mourn? What would it mean to stand with them in faith that they "will be comforted"?

As you reread the verses, listen with your heart. For whom is God calling you to be an Isaiah? To whom do you need to speak or to be God's comfort? Name them in your journal and lift them to God in love. Consider how to "speak tenderly" to them in Christ's name as opportunities arise. Be open to God's direction.

As you read or hear about news events and go about your daily affairs during the next day, carry within you the words of verse 1, "Comfort, O comfort my people.…" Open your heart to the sorrow of those around you. Write of your experience.

EXERCISE 3   MOURNING OUR SIN, TURNING TO GOD

Read Joel 1:8-15; 2:12-14. For the prophet Joel, mourning is not only a feeling; it is an active and necessary lamenting of our sin in the course of returning to the Lord. Read the passage aloud several times with feeling. Listen to the pathos in Joel's call to return to the Lord "with all your heart, with fasting, with weeping, and with mourning."

As you read, get in touch with a need for spiritual recovery "while [the Lord] may be found" (Isa. 55:6), that is, while there is still time. In your journal and as an exercise only, write a confidential letter to someone you trust confessing your need to return to the Lord. Describe the active mourning and releasing that you will need to undergo.

Dwell prayerfully on Joel 2:13-14. Consider how you might embody God's gracious nature for someone else as part of your "return to the Lord." What blessing might you and the Lord leave behind for him or her (2:14)?

EXERCISE 4   MOVING FROM GRIEF TO JOY

Read John 16:20-22. In this passage, Jesus prepares his disciples for his death by giving them a comforting image with which to mourn, an image of suffering followed by joy. Think about all the ways this image actually fits the disciples' stories. When has this image matched your experience?

What other images or metaphors do you find helpful and hopeful in the midst of mourning loss of any kind? What images do you find especially unhelpful?

Take to God a loss or sorrow that is weighing on you. Listen to what God is saying to you through Jesus' words.

Pray for someone who is mourning.

EXERCISE 5   WEEPING WITH JESUS

Read Luke 19:41-44 (see 13:34-35). In this passage, we witness Jesus weeping with compassion for Jerusalem, the city of peace, and mourning its refusal to recognize "the things that make for peace." Return to verse 41 and meditate on it: "As he came near and saw the city, he wept over it." Enter imaginatively into what Jesus saw and the grief he felt.

Where would you imagine Jesus weeping today in your community? Jot down places as they come to mind. In each setting consider what kingdom possibility Jesus is weeping for.

Pick one of the settings that came to mind and sit with Jesus in prayer. Enter imaginatively into the concern and the hope that Jesus would bring to the situation. Converse with Jesus about what "they will be comforted" means for this place, these people, and for you.

Record your insights.

Remember to review the insights recorded in your notebook or journal for the week in preparation for the group meeting.

Week 4

The Power of a Clear and Gentle Heart

"Blessed are the meek, for they will inherit the earth."

In the popular musical *Camelot*, King Arthur's illegitimate son, Mordred, dishes up a satirical song called "The Seven Deadly Virtues." With comedic sarcasm he sings, "It's not the earth the meek inherit, it's the dirt!"[1] Those who consider themselves realists would no doubt agree. The world has its own creed, which goes something like this: "Blessed are the self-assertive and intimidating, for they shall get whatever they want."[2] The world holds a crude faith in external power. On the surface it is the mighty, the wealthy, the ruthless who own the earth and plunder its resources for gain and fame. For thousands of years the powerful have exploited cheap labor, building private fortunes and political empires on the backs of those with little voice. The high and mighty may reason that God can give heaven to the poor, the sad, or the meek, so long as the earth is reserved for those who take it by force.

The "earth" we speak of here is the fallen world, a world in the grip of "the cosmic powers of this present darkness" (Eph. 6:12) in which we all participate. Jesus is revealing to us another world, the realm of God's reign that operates on very different principles. The kingdom of God is the new spiritual order, in and from which Jesus already lives. He invites us to enter the joyful realm of this order even in the midst of this world. But we have trouble comprehending God's realm, so our desire for it is often dim.

For example, we don't understand the notion of meekness very well. Like *humble*, a closely related word, *meek* brings to mind unhelpful connotations: images of blandness and impotence. Meek translates as "weak" in our culture. We will not teach our children meekness because we fear they will become passive doormats for aggressive kids. We do not reward meekness in business because we value tough-minded action in a fiercely competitive free market. Our culture worships power in all its forms—from status and money to military and civilian weapons, from physical strength and seductive attraction to unlimited gas and electricity, from privileged information and knowledge to ever-increasing computer speed and stereo volume. We are "into" power, not humility. Even our TVs and VCRs feature "power switches" rather than mere "On/Off" buttons. We enjoy the sensation of exercising power.[3]

Our first step into this beatitude is to revisit the meaning of true meekness. Grasping its meaning will in turn help us reconsider the nature and blessing of authentic power. Then we can explore the relation of meekness to "inheriting the earth" and how this connection reveals the reign of God.

True Meekness

We tend to think of meekness in negative terms, as lack of spine or colorless character. Nothing could be further from its meaning. In English translations, scripture uses the word *meek* to describe only two individuals: Moses and Jesus, the character giants of both Hebrew and Christian scriptures.

One writer notes, "Biblical meekness seems closer to the gentleness of a lioness with her cubs than to the hesitancy of a mouse cowering before a cat!"[4] Moses was indeed a lion to the people of Israel. This prince of Egypt who fled to far-off Midian after killing a cruel master of the Hebrew slaves could not retreat among the sheep forever. God called him to lead the Hebrew people out of slavery. Through forty years of wilderness wandering, Moses guided them to the brink of the new land God had promised. Moses, while an icon of strength as a leader, was "very meek, above all…which were upon the face of the earth" (Num. 12:3, KJV).

In this passage, the Hebrew word translated "meek" (King James Version) can also be translated "humble" (New Revised Standard Version). It could even be rendered "devout." The range of related meanings is instructive. Both humble and meek are translations of the Hebrew term *anav*, which indicates lack of status. The *anawim* (plural) referred to the poor, the humble, those without status in the social hierarchy. How curious that Moses, cited as the greatest leader of Israel, is considered *anav*. Yet he embodied what his own people were—"no people"—except that God called them out of nothing to be a nation, not for their own sake but as "a light to the nations."

Jesus actually describes himself as meek: "Take my yoke upon you, and learn of me, for I am meek and lowly in heart" (Matt. 11: 29, KJV). Another translation says, "I am gentle and humble in heart." According to some scholars, the Greek word means "gentle but strong." It suggests "strength that is under control and tinged with a spirit of caring."[5] Jesus identifies with the *anawim* of Israel, those without status. He also connects the gentleness and humility of his heart with "rest for your souls." Can gentleness provide a restful way through this world as we are willingly yoked with Jesus' purpose and path?

It is curious that Jesus would speak of meekness as restful, given his own suffering under those opposed to the kind of kingdom he preached. Jesus promised his disciples that they too would suffer if they followed him, because the world could not abide what their lives represented. The cross looks anything but restful; it looks like a sign of victimization at the hands of the powerful. And this is just where we fear gentleness, humility, and meekness will get us: victimized.

Later in the Sermon on the Mount, Jesus seems to reinforce the idea of becoming a voluntary victim. He teaches his followers not to resist an evildoer (Matt. 5:38-42). Indeed, he gives three examples of not resisting: turning the other cheek, giving more than asked for in a law suit, and walking a second mile. This is hard advice to swallow, especially for those of us who expect to exercise a certain amount of control over our lives. It seems Jesus is allowing others to

> *Yielding to the benevolent purposes of God prepares us for the yoke of kind, gentle, patient service to others.*
>
> —John S. Mogabgab

be irresponsible and teaching us not to hold them accountable for their behavior. Again, if we don't understand the context of Jesus' time we will miss the revolutionary force of his words.

Our Powers at God's Disposal

Let us explore briefly the work of Bible scholar Walter Wink who brilliantly illuminates the original context and intended meaning of Jesus' teachings in Matthew 5:38-42. First, let's be clear that Jesus' primary audience was "the poor," the lower rungs of the social strata who were dominated by secular and religious rulers. Next, let's identify with the "you" in these teachings. Notice that in his first illustration Jesus specifies "the right cheek." This would require someone to strike you with the back of the right hand, since the left hand was used only for "unclean" tasks. A back-handed slap was a serious insult and a routine way to keep inferiors in line. By turning the other cheek, you are serving notice that you refuse to be humiliated. To strike the left cheek would require the person striking you to use the palm of the right hand, a sign that you are a person of equal worth.

The second illustration is set in a court of law. The poor lived under terrible burdens of debt in Jesus' time, often losing everything they had to repay their creditors. Jewish law strictly forbade creditors to keep past sundown a poor person's outer garment as a pledge of repayment, since it might be the only item the person had to sleep in (see Exod. 22:25-27; Deut. 24:10-13, 17). In addition, Jewish custom considered nakedness a great shame for those viewing or causing nakedness rather than for the naked person. So by giving the creditor your undergarment as well as outer garment, leaving yourself naked, you essentially expose the injustice of the whole debt system and leave your creditors covered with shame.

Finally, soldiers were allowed by Roman law to force civilians to carry their heavy equipment packs for no more than one mile, with stiff penalties for soldiers who exceeded the limit. If you willingly offer to carry such a pack more than a mile, you throw the soldier into significant discomfort. In the words of Walter Wink: "Imagine the situation of a Roman infantryman pleading with a Jew to give back his pack!"[6]

Jesus wants you, as one of his listeners, to be so clear about your value in God's eyes that you can imagine taking initiative away from someone "above you" in the social hierarchy and taking back the power of choice. Jesus has given you a practical way to recover your humanity in a world that despises the many and exalts the few. These examples do more than illustrate "not resisting evildoers"; they reveal what Jesus means by "meekness." Having true meekness bears no resemblance to being a cringing doormat. Meekness is, rather, the subversive power of "loving our enemies," the potential to transform others by the clarity of our own transformed attitudes and actions. Meekness is the strong gentleness of power under control—the control of God's Spirit.

When a horse allows itself to be saddled, ridden, and directed by a rider, we say it is "gentled." To gentle a horse implies a relationship in which the horse's power comes under human control. The horse's power is not taken away or diminished, but it can become as gentle as Danny, a farm horse who allows little two-year-old Lex to ride on his back in perfect safety, even while his strength and speed help Lex's father accomplish daily farm tasks. Meekness is human strength under God's direction. All of us have powers—intelligence, skills, energy, emotions, and speech. The great question of human life and meaning has to do with how we use our powers and for what purpose. We need to be "gentled" by God so that our powers are at the disposal of divine purpose.

Jesus himself used his powers solely at God's discretion—sometimes in direct action and sometimes in refraining from action. In the wilderness, Jesus used his deep knowledge of scripture to refute the devil who tried three times to seduce him with worldly expressions of power. Later, in a dramatic witness to the power of God in him, Jesus drove demons into a pig herd that promptly plunged off a cliff. Another time, after preaching an unpopular message in his hometown, he merely passed through the angry mob that was ready to throw him off a cliff! Innumerable times, when challenged to use his

I have tried in every way…to make myself what I know I ought to be, but have always failed. Now I give it up to thee.…Work in me all the good pleasure of thy will.

—Hannah Whitall Smith

remarkable powers to prove himself to skeptics, he refused. He did not waste his energy trying to defend, justify, or protect himself. Finally in Gethsemane he allowed himself to be arrested and taken before the authorities, subject to God in the use of all his powers. Clarence Jordan's words capture the essence of Jesus' powerful meekness:

> People may be called "meek" to the extent that they have surrendered their wills to God and learned to do God's bidding....the secret to the power of the meek [is]....that *God's will becomes their will.* Whoever fights them is fighting against God, for a surrendered human will is the agency through which God's power is released upon the earth.[7]

Inheriting the Earth

How does this clear and gentle strength, this power surrendered to divine love, connect with inheriting the earth? The concept is not new in the Hebrew tradition. In this beatitude Jesus echoes Psalm 37:11: "But the meek shall inherit the land, and delight themselves in abundant prosperity."

The psalmist observed that all the wrong people prospered, which directly contradicted the older Hebrew view that material prosperity came to those faithful to God's commands. So the psalmist looked ahead to God's future and saw that those who waited patiently for the Lord to act would receive vindication. Those who refrained from anger or vengeance, who trusted God and committed their ways to the Lord, would see the wicked vanish like smoke. Indignation was wasted energy. The Lord simply laughed at the pretenses and ambitions of the wicked; and, in the long view, so should the faithful. Psalm 37 is a promise for patient believers.

This beatitude is also set in future tense: The meek *will* inherit the earth. It is not an obvious truth. The movers and shakers of this world find the whole notion laughably absurd. But the humble and gentle-hearted find laughable the presumptions and confidence of the mighty. Tyrants have a way of digging their own graves and eventually falling into them. There is nothing substantial or lasting in ambition and

Time, rather than power, is on the side of the righteous.

—Simon Tugwell

wealth. The earth and its gifts belong finally to those who wait and trust, whose wills are given over in joyful abandon to God.

As the psalmist and Jesus put it so clearly, the earth is an inheritance from God; no one can possess it except as a gift from God. An inheritance is not earned or achieved but received. We do not receive it because of our intelligence, wealth, or worthiness but because we are sons and daughters of the One who has all to offer. We begin to come into our inheritance as we show ourselves to be sons and daughters, sharing God's humility, love, and freedom to serve others.

Moreover, "possession" of the earth is not finally a matter of title deeds, walls, and fences. An artist who sees and renders the beauty in a landscape possesses the earth. The child who knows creation to be filled with the glory of God possesses the earth.

A forest ranger once commented, "If you walk into the forest quietly, stilling your mind, not taking up any more space than you really need, noticing and being respectful of the life around you, the animals recognize you as one of their own, and treat you accordingly."[8] To walk through the world this way, gently, not imposing yourself, is to possess the earth—an interior and spiritual possession more true and powerful than the holding of any deed. And possessing the earth in this way expresses a heart already given to God's realm and reign.

The humble and gentle know who and whose they are. They do not see themselves as greater or lesser than they are. Being poor in spirit, they know how entirely their lives and good depend on God. They respect all that belongs to God, every creature that shares this earth. Thus they are its natural heirs.[9] Those who live in the strong but gentle power of meekness live already by the values and principles of God's kingdom. They allow divine will and love to reign in their hearts and lives. They already "possess the earth" in the deepest and most abiding sense. But the promise of this beatitude has a future fulfillment we can only dimly imagine. The meek will inherit the earth. What this means in the fullness of God's kingdom will surely be a joy to see. Imagine an earth wisely governed by those who are truly humble-hearted, clear-minded, God-centered, and full of gentle strength. Surely this would be the reign of God among us!

> *A man might buy up a continent and never possess a square foot of it.*
> —Percy C. Ainsworth

DAILY EXERCISES

This week's reading reminds us that meekness is seldom an attribute we seek for ourselves or admire in others. Yet Jesus and Moses are both described as "meek." Read Week Four, "The Power of a Clear and Gentle Heart." Then note your thoughts in your journal. As you move through this week's daily exercises, seek to discover the strength in meekness that comes to those who allow God to direct their lives. As you begin each reflection time, take a moment to center yourself. Relax your body. Empty your mind of distractions, and invite God to help you grow in meekness.

We turn toward God, from whom we have come, upon whom we depend for our being, and to whom we will return.

—Ben Campbell Johnson

EXERCISE 1   LISTENING TO JESUS

Read Matthew 4:23–5:5. Explore your various images of meekness. Which images fit or don't fit your perceptions of what Jesus was like?

As you listen to Jesus' words, consider the persons in your community they bring to mind. Lift those persons to God and bless them. Pay attention to where Jesus' blessing both affirms and challenges you.

Identify one person you would call meek in a manner that Jesus would applaud. Describe the characteristics you see. Is this the kind of person that you hope will inherit the earth? How would tomorrow be different if that were to happen today? Pull together your thoughts by writing your own paraphrase of the beatitude.

Practice an awareness of God's gentle guiding presence throughout the next twenty-four hours. Watch for "the meek" and bless them with a prayer of thanks for the grace in them. Describe what you see in your journal.

EXERCISE 2   BEING STRONG UNDER GOD'S DIRECTION

Read Numbers 12:1-8. Numbers describes Moses, the powerful leader who led the Hebrews out of slavery, as "very meek, above all…which were upon the face of the earth" (KJV). Perhaps in this obscure story, Moses illustrates "the strong gentleness of power under…the control of God's spirit" in his relationship with Miriam and Aaron.

Focus on the action in verse 1. Recall a time when someone spoke against you as Miriam and Aaron spoke against Moses. How did you react? Did you react harshly, become a doormat, or respond with the gentle strength of love? Reflect on what it means for you to be strong in gentleness and humility within the direction of God's love.

Enter into a face-to-face time with God. Bring to mind people who aggravate you. Allow God's presence to "gentle" your reactive feelings. Practice God's gentling presence in preparation for your next encounter with them. Record your experience.

EXERCISE 3 TAKING CHRIST'S YOKE

Read Matthew 11:28-30 three times, practicing a form of *lectio divina*. The first time through, pay attention to words and images that draw you, such as "you that are weary" or "take my yoke upon you, and learn from me." Jot them down in your journal and ponder what may have drawn you to these phrases.

With the second reading, listen prayerfully to what touches you or connects with you in some way. For instance, you might imagine the yoke as the double yoke of a pair of work oxen. What would it be like to yoke your life with Christ, allowing him to share your load and learning his way of working through a trying situation?

With the third reading, pay attention to the invitation or call you hear. Perhaps it is to "learn from" Christ a new way of relating to your family members or coworkers. Pray for sensitivity to follow the grace and guidance of the Christ within.

EXERCISE 4 WILLING GOD'S WILL

Read Luke 1:26-38. While Mary is *anav* (the meek of the land), she also models interior meekness in her surrender to God that yields an inheritance for all. After reading the passage through once, read it meditatively, entering imaginatively into Mary's experience. With each verse, pause to visualize what is happening and to consider how you would feel and respond in Mary's situation. Capture your experience in your journal.

Remain with verse 38 and take up Mary's response to God as a prayer of complete surrender: "Here am I, the servant of the Lord;

let it be with me according to your word." Repeat it slowly and ponder what you are saying to God. Each time you breathe, say the prayer again: inhaling "Here am I…" and exhaling "let it be with me…." Stay with this prayer for a few minutes.

Reflect in your journal on your experience with Mary's prayer and meekness before God.

EXERCISE 5   LETTING THE LORD GENTLE AND GUIDE YOU

Read Acts 9:1-31. The image from the week's reading of a horse "being gentled" describes the change that began in Paul on the road to Damascus. How do you see the Lord "gentling" this strong-willed Pharisee?

Reflect on some ways that the Lord has "gentled" you over the course of your life, making you more meek and willing as a servant of God. In what ways and under what circumstances are you still "bucking"?

Imagine yourself as a beautiful Thoroughbred for the Lord. Give yourself fully to your Master's commands, trusting the Master's direction and mission. Be sensitive to the Master's slightest prompting to turn this way or that way in the mission of life. Where and to whom would the Lord have you go? In what settings do you find yourself?

Remember to review the insights recorded in your notebook or journal for the week in preparation for the group meeting.

Week 5

A Satisfying Hunger and Thirst

"Blessed are those who hunger and thirst for righteousness,
for they will be filled."

H ave you ever known serious hunger or thirst? Some of us, perhaps, have lived through situations that have brought us face-to-face with these elemental forces of physical life. If so, we know that real hunger brings wrenching pain and increasing weakness. We know that true thirst is an all-consuming need. Hunger and thirst drive us to find a way to fill the void with food and drink.

In our largely middle-class Western culture, saturated with food and drink of every kind, it is difficult to imagine the imperatives of hunger and thirst that so many people in this world know. Yet we have brief encounters that give us a taste of the full reality. Perhaps in our busyness we forget to eat a meal, and pangs of hunger begin to stab at us. Perhaps in the preparation and aftermath of surgery we experience the cotton-dry mouth and parched throat of thirst.

In my early twenties at the peak of my physical strength, I once set out on a hiking trek with two companions in an arid region of New Mexico. We foolishly failed to bring more than one canteen of water each and were forced to return to home base long before we reached our intended destination. I had never known such parchedness and physical fatigue. One of my companions, near fainting, required the support of the two others toward the end, which added to our exhaustion. When we finally got back to the ranch I remember consuming a full pitcher of water, scarcely stopping to breathe and two more

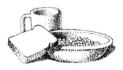

pitchers within the next fifteen minutes. I had never realized that I could physically consume that much water or that my body could absorb it. It was my first and only experience of serious dehydration.

Hungering and Thirsting for Righteousness

The people who listened to Jesus' Sermon on the Mount knew the physical realities of hunger and thirst. They lived with uncertain crop harvests in an arid region of the earth. Water was a precious resource in centers of human population surrounded by desert. Jesus applied their experience of hunger and thirst to a spiritual need as real and great as physical nourishment: "Happy are those who hunger and thirst for righteousness; they shall be fully satisfied."

Righteousness has become an overused and little understood term. It may seem antiquated or feel moralistic. Many "good religious folks" who consider themselves righteous are, in truth, self-righteous. Sometimes our governments engage in actions justified as righteous when we deeply suspect they too are being self-righteous. Understood moralistically, this word is a problem.

We tend to narrow righteousness to external rules and regulations, filling its meaning with whatever we believe is the morally or ethically correct thing to do. In our recent history, righteousness has meant everything from not offending polite society to not dancing or playing cards. In Jesus' time, righteousness meant attending and contributing to the Temple and obeying hundreds of rules, precepts, traditions, and laws. While righteousness was considered necessary, no one enjoyed it; only the religious elite (scribes, Pharisees, priests) were thought to really do it right. Such "righteousness" was external, motivated by the reward of human praise. It was, as Jesus accurately saw, an imitation piety with no power whatsoever to glorify God or to satisfy the human soul.

What then is an authentic understanding of righteousness, one that can fill our deepest spiritual hunger and thirst? One spiritual writer declares, "Righteousness is the fulfillment of God's creative purpose in a [person's] whole life."[1] Another describes it as the "total

> *Do not be afraid that the Lord Who has called us to drink of this spring will allow us to die of thirst.*
>
> —Teresa of Ávila

right order" of God's kingdom, "including the right ordering of our lives."[2] Thus the personal dimension of righteousness contributes to an overarching social reality of righteousness. The "total right order" is God's intended reign in human affairs at every level, which cannot come to full light without the participation of every human being.

Those of us with genuine faith and the spark of Christ's hope in our hearts do hunger and thirst for God's right ordering of life. We yearn for an order of life in which people treat others fairly and generously, where no one goes to bed hungry and children do not die from preventable diseases. We thirst for a sense of justice to pervade the choices and actions of all people, especially the powerful. We hunger for the earth to be spared from our own destructiveness, so that its beauty and abundance might be available to our children, grandchildren, and many further generations to come.

Christianity [is] a community of mutual need and nourishment whose very life… is sustained by its continuous feeding of one another and being fed.
—Wendy M. Wright

The Promise of Full Satisfaction

Yet again we feel the paradox of Jesus' words. The idea that those who hunger and thirst for righteousness receive deep satisfaction does not seem to square with reality. Those who seek justice for the weak seem always at the margins of society; those who make valiant efforts toward peace rarely win the day; those who are passionate about the way of God in this competitive and self-serving world seem to face one obstacle after another. Goodness often gets the short end of the stick and sometimes seems swallowed up in the scramble for power. Our yearning for the right ordering of life—within ourselves, our communities, our nation, our world—seldom finds deep or lasting satisfaction in visible results. The ills of this world, on the other hand, are altogether visible. Apparently this is an old problem! Many Jews in the days before Jesus' time seem to have concluded: "Now we count the arrogant happy; evildoers not only prosper, but when they put God to the test they escape" (Mal. 3:15).

Even more disconcerting, those things that appear to be good and right at the start often show themselves later to be ineffective or corrupt. Good intentions can go awry through greed, naivete, or sheer ignorance. We send food aid to starving people, and it rots on the docks of countries paralyzed by political infighting or lack of a delivery infrastructure. We send infant formula to poor mothers in developing countries, and their babies die from infection because the mothers have no way to sterilize bottles. How easily we could despair of our efforts!

Yet Jesus says unequivocally that when we hunger and thirst for God's rightly ordered reign we will be blessed with full satisfaction. In this beatitude, the sense of the word translated "filled" is more like "stuffed full." Jesus describes this same quality with the phrase, "A good measure, pressed down, shaken together, running over…" when he speaks of receiving the measure we give to others (Luke 6:38). The joy and blessing of God's reign exceed our highest expectations and most vivid imagination!

Are we then to take Jesus' words as a promise for the distant future, a satisfaction to be received "when kingdom comes"? Not entirely, although the fullness of his promise belongs to the world to come. The scriptures are full of "last days" promises that come with God's judgment and final establishment of justice, purity, and peace. Responding to those Jews who "count the arrogant happy," Malachi assures them there will be a day when the arrogant will be left "neither root nor branch" (just as the psalmist in Psalm 37 proclaims that no sign of the wicked will be left on earth when the meek inherit it). Malachi continues, "But for you who revere my name the sun of righteousness shall rise, with healing in its wings" (4:2). Here is a promise for a future we can barely perceive. Yet this promise is present tense as well, and it belongs to the appetite for righteousness.

Our Hunger for God, God's Hunger for Us

Our thirst for loving, just, rightly ordered relationships in our lives and world expresses our thirst for God. Hunger for the ways of God expresses hunger for the source of these ways. Just as hunger and thirst are elemental to our physical life, so hunger and thirst for God are fundamental to our spiritual life.

Our inner doors open and light enters when we acknowledge our hunger for God, and begin the quest for God.

—Ronald S. James

As a deer longs for flowing streams,
    so my soul longs for you, O God.
My soul thirsts for God,
    for the living God.
When shall I come and behold
    the face of God? (Ps. 42:1-2)

We cannot live without God. Our souls yearn for God with bitter-sweet longing as exiles yearn for a beloved home they but dimly remember. We are all hollowness and deficiency without God, for God alone gives us a real and solid identity. Once again we find ourselves on the ground of spiritual poverty. God did not create us to be independent but rather for a life of deep and joyous communion with God, with other human beings, and with the whole creation. If we reject our spiritual poverty instead of embracing it, how can God take the chalice of our receptivity and fill it with the magnificent happiness of this communion?

In trying to provide our own meaning, purpose, and enjoyment in life, we merely end up making ourselves miserable. We settle for "trinkets when we wanted a kingdom."[3] We divert our hunger and thirst to a thousand lesser things that cannot make us happy. We think we want food when we really want love. We imagine that sexual freedom will help us to feel lovable. We want a relationship that can meet all our needs, but no one can bear the weight of our need for God. Our desires are global and infinite. We want fashionable clothes, high-tech gadgets, the good opinion of others, high-achieving children, annual salary increases, the "right" political candidate, security, popularity, and power. But we may reap great unhappiness if we fall prey to all our wants! Observe the lives of the rich and famous, people who can often command their wishes to be granted. Are they happy people? Just look at the incidence of drug and alcohol addiction, the intensity of jealousy and rivalry, the feelings of insecurity and worthlessness that run so high even among the most privileged of this world. Fascinating fads and the temporary glitter of glory do not have enough substance to give us true happiness.

Within us all there is a yearning that nothing—no thing, no created object, no person, no pleasure—can satisfy. We are athirst for the living God.

—David Rensberger

God has made us in such a way that our hearts can only be truly satisfied by participating in the life of God. Our highest bliss comes from going out of ourselves in love to God, others, and to all creatures. We could say that our greatest joy is to allow the life of God's self-giving love to live through us.

Jesus tells us to "strive first for the kingdom of God" and divine righteousness; all our other needs and desires will fall into place around this central priority (Matt. 6:33). When we give full rein to our basic appetite for God, it orders other appetites in life so that we can enjoy them without needing to grasp for them. Then we begin to receive life as gift and understand the meaning of gratitude. Do you know that God has "hard-wired" you to desire goodness even though you can resist and choose against it? The appetite for God and life in God remain our most fundamental hunger. Nothing else can satisfy it, and our souls accept no substitute. Pale idols may cloud our minds, but our souls recognize counterfeit gods.

Thirst for God is a lodestone of holy yearning that draws us into the caverns of the heart and the byways of the world seeking the only One who can relieve our privation.

—John S. Mogabgab

Righteousness "is the human spirit recognizing and claiming its kinship with [God], and seeking all that is involved in that relationship."[4] We find in this relationship everything that is right in life, all we are meant to be in God. Moreover our personal thirst for God is met by God's gracious spirit welling up and "overflowing into the thirsty world around us, so that our thirst for God's will, our thirst 'to see right prevail' in that world, can find satisfaction as the world itself drinks in the love of God."[5] Hunger for both personal and social righteousness go hand in hand and are filled together.

An important point: Our hungering thirst for God and for divine righteousness is a mere shadow of God's hunger and thirst for us. God suffers a terrible yearning for restored communion with wayward human creatures. So the Spirit beckons us toward the fullness of God's reign. We do not have our own righteousness, only what God gives us. We cannot achieve the right order of things by our own cleverness, energy, or goodwill. Christ our righteousness provides a mature example of the right order of God's kingdom. Jesus is God's gift to us to help restore the communion of God's reign. As we faithfully live in him and abide in his spirit, his righteousness becomes our own. Christ can give himself to those who consciously acknowledge their spiritual poverty, who are gentle-hearted and humble, and who truly mourn the state of the world and their own complicity in its illusions. In Jesus, God "comes to us as food and as fountain."[6] "I am the bread of life. Whoever comes to me will never be hungry, and whoever believes in me will never be thirsty" (John 6:35).

Even now the promise is fulfilled for us to this degree: As we hunger and thirst for God's own life and truth, we will know deep satisfaction. We will feel ourselves "at one with the profoundest laws of [our] spiritual being"[7] and know we are reconciled to the very best within us. This reconciliation makes all that we do in every season of our lives significant and constructive. Righteousness is available to all who deeply and genuinely desire it. God responds to our hunger for the divine presence and our thirst for divine will. For this we were made. To ensure that we could receive it God came to us in person!

DAILY EXERCISES

This week our journey through the beatitudes moves to a new level. Thus far, Jesus' blessings give us faith to come before God with our need, to express the depth of our concern, and to surrender to God's will. With this beatitude, Jesus invites us to embrace our longing for God's promises—the kingdom of heaven on earth, in us and among us. Read Week Five, "A Satisfying Hunger and Thirst," and record your thoughts in your journal. As you approach each of the daily exercises that follow, pray that you will discover God's invitation for your life.

EXERCISE 1 LISTENING TO JESUS

Read Matthew 5:6. What persons or groups of people come to mind when you think of "those who hunger and thirst for righteousness" in your world, community, or church? List them and circle the ones whose qualities whet your appetite for righteousness or for justice. Name the qualities that stir your hunger and thirst for what's right.

In light of your reflections on "those who hunger and thirst," write a paraphrase of the beatitude.

Let your "hunger and thirst" for what's right and just be your prayer. Offer your yearning to God and rest in the promise that you "will be filled." Capture your prayer in your journal.

EXERCISE 2 PRAYING FOR THE KINGDOM

Read Matthew 6:9-13. In this Gospel account, Jesus teaches what we call the Lord's Prayer right in the middle of his sermon on a higher righteousness. This prayer grounds that higher righteousness in a relationship with "our Father in heaven," a longing for "your kingdom come," and a readiness to do "your will" here and now "on earth as it is in heaven."

As you pray this prayer, pause after each phrase to be in genuine relationship with God and to speak your heart. As you pray, "Our Father…," acknowledge God's presence; remember who and whose you are.

As you pray "Your kingdom come," bring to mind God's dream for life in your family, church, community, and world. Imagine what Jesus would bless, address, or mend in those settings.

As you pray "Your will be done, on earth as it is in heaven," say yes to God's dream. Offer yourself to be an instrument of God's will. Pray, "your will be done" in _____ (name specific settings), making yourself available to God.

Close by praying the remainder of the Lord's Prayer.

EXERCISE 3   ORDERING OUR LIVES RIGHTLY

Read Micah 6:6-8. What does righteousness require? It is not found in external sacrifices and obligations. Righteousness is "to do justice, and to love kindness, and to walk humbly with your God."

To aid your reflection, draw a triangle (or three interlocking circles) and above it write, "what is good." Beside each of the three sides (or within each of the interlocking circles), write one of the three phrases from Micah. Ponder your triangle as an image of the righteous life that Jesus calls for and three key disciplines for living it. Reflect on it in your journal.

Review the past week of your life through the lens of this image and these three ways of practicing "what is good." Jot down recollections of where you practiced or failed to practice any of the three disciplines for living what God requires.

Close in a time of prayer, expressing your hunger and thirst for God and the good life that Christ came to give us.

EXERCISE 4   OVERFLOWING INTO A THIRSTY WORLD

Read John 7:37-39. To Jesus' words, David Rensberger responds:

> The Spirit welling up within us is capable of overflowing into the thirsty world around us, so that our thirst for God's will, our thirst "to see right prevail' in that world, can find satisfaction as the world itself drinks in the love of God."[8]

This passage reminds us that the righteousness we seek was fulfilled in Jesus' life and that Jesus' life comes alive in us through the gift of

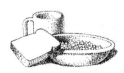

the Spirit. Close your eyes and come to Jesus in prayer. Open your thirsty soul to the Spirit of the living God flowing through Jesus like rivers of fresh, pure water. Drink deeply from the waters and allow the waters that fill you to flow out of your heart to thirsty places in relationships and places around you. Keep your prayer focus for a while by reciting with Jesus, "Out of the believer's heart shall flow rivers of living water."

Record your experience and reflect on these questions. What does it mean for you to stay in the flow? What are the dry places in you that need a good soaking if you would live in and live out the love of Jesus? Who are the thirsty people that will benefit when the waters of life flow through you?

EXERCISE 5   LIVING IN THE SPIRIT OF THE LORD

Read Luke 4:16-19, 20-30. In reading this passage from Isaiah (61:1-2), Jesus announces the saving mission that the Spirit empowers and sends him to fulfill. Write out each distinct phrase of the mission statement. Meditate on each, one at a time. Search out the meaning of each phrase. Make notes on your thoughts and questions.

Look over the phrases. Which ones make you especially hungry for a time when things are set right regarding certain people or situations? What do these phrases mean to you?

Let one phrase choose you. Explore how Jesus fulfilled that assignment in his day and how you might participate in fulfilling it today. Pray, "The Spirit of the Lord is upon me, to _____," filling in the blank with the need or assignment that has chosen you. Ask the Spirit of the Lord to help you see something you can do over the next day to acknowledge this prompting and to share joyfully in the fulfillment of God's promise for people. Record your experience.

Remember to review the insights recorded in your notebook or journal for the week in preparation for the group meeting.

Week 6

Embracing the Wisdom of Tenderness

"Blessed are the merciful,
for they will receive mercy."

$\mathcal{E}$dward Farrell went to Ireland to help his favorite uncle celebrate his eightieth birthday. On the morning of the great day, they got up early and watched the sun rise over Lake Killarney. For twenty minutes they stood in complete silence until his uncle began skipping along the shore with a radiant smile. "Can you tell me why you are so happy?" asked Ed. "Yes, lad," the old man replied, tears streaming down his face. "You see, the Father is very fond of me. Ah, me Father is so very fond of me."[1]

Do you believe that God is truly fond of you? If so, you have accepted the truth of divine tenderness. The scriptures reveal the compassionate heart of God. "By the tender mercy of our God, the dawn from on high will break upon us, to give light to those who sit in darkness and in the shadow of death, to guide our feet into the way of peace" (Luke 1:78-79). "The tenderness and love of God our Savior has dawned in our lives; he saved us not because of any righteous deeds we had done but because of his mercy" (Titus 3:4-5, JB). Tender compassion and mercy are God's deepest nature . We see them in the face of Jesus Christ, and we hear them in his teachings.

This beatitude calls us to participate in the mercy God shows, thereby receiving the fullness of its blessing. We are more inclined to embrace this beatitude without argument, for it fits our sense of fairness. There is a softness, a healing balm in these words that puts

We are judged, not by some extrinsic measure, but simply by the truth of what we are in God's making.
—Simon Tugwell

65

our hearts at ease and gives us hope for humanity. But that doesn't mean we find it easy to be merciful as God is merciful. It takes time, struggle, and a great deal of grace to learn to love as God loves.

Hunger and thirst for righteousness can lead to unkind feelings toward the unjust. It is probably no accident that a reminder to be merciful follows immediately on the beatitude concerning our yearning for justice. It is as if Jesus says, "You may not allow zeal for right order to make you ungenerous and judgmental." God's project in the face of human sin is conversion and redemption for all people, oppressed and oppressor alike. Those of us who have learned to hunger for the divine right order are to be like God in this hope, to join God in the great creative scheme of redeeming love. For to be honest, God is very fond of all of us, regardless of how far we have fallen from the divine image!

Through this gift of forgiveness, God throws away the score-card and declares that everyone wins.

—Rodger Nishioka
Judy Kuo

Entering God's Mercy

The depth of God's mercy forms the only true basis for ours. Divine mercy releases us, disentangles us from the sticky web of sin, freeing us to choose God's reign again. Mercy is part of God's right order, a centerpiece of kingdom truth. Yet we tend to think of mercy and justice as opposed to each other or at least locked in serious tension.

In our typical frame of reference, mercy is simply the "softening agent" in the hard, cold waters of justice; the touch of leniency in the judge's sentence. But in God's frame of reference, mercy and justice weave the warp and woof of one fabric—part of the just order of God's reign. Thérèse of Lisieux, one of the great saints of the church, wrote, "What joy to think that God is just, that he takes account of our weaknesses, that he knows perfectly the fragility of our nature."[2] On the other hand, mercy as part of divine justice does not simply let us off the hook for wrongdoing. God loves us too much to offer cheap and ineffectual grace. We suffer the consequences of our sin, yet in a way that gives us opportunity to see and live differently if we choose. Mercy is tenaciously strong, flexible, and realistic. There is indeed great wisdom in this tenderness.

God's mercy, though a divine attribute and activity, draws us in as participants. Through it, Jesus calls us to enter God's central character trait—love. Jesus urges us to embrace it, to enlarge its healing influence in the world. These actions show that we are indeed God's children, heirs, and images. When we look at Luke's Gospel, we see this emphasis on relationship more clearly:

> "But I say to you that listen, Love your enemies, do good to those who hate you, bless those who curse you, pray for those who abuse you…. Your reward will be great, and you will be children of the Most High; for he is kind to the ungrateful and the wicked. Be merciful, just as your Father is merciful." (Luke 6:27-28, 35-36)

Scripture continually affirms the mercy of God. The Hebrew term *hesed* is often translated "loving-kindness." Cousins of this term include kinship love, compassion, and tender mercy. *Hesed* is the chief characteristic of the God we know best in the life and person of Jesus.

But to be merciful as our God is merciful means we must know our own need for mercy above all else. It avails us little to imagine that our sins are somehow less serious than those of others or more serious for that matter. Comparisons of sin are specious, since we are all in the same sinking boat. To see the truth of who God made us to be is to see both our utter brokenness and the possibility of our full recovery. And we see these twin truths not just for ourselves but for every human being, since all are created in the divine image. We can exclude no one from the possibility of new life by God's grace. People can and do change. God's word has "inexhaustible power to bring life out of death, perfection out of disaster…being out of non-being."[3]

Jesus fully understands the foolishness of our comparative judgments. He points out the hypocrisy of removing the speck from our neighbor's eye while peering out from eyes obstructed by a log! Our comparison of sins reveals our folly. The log in our eye is not the "size" of our sin but our lack of humility and love toward our neighbor. With this huge impediment, we cannot possibly see clearly enough to judge our neighbor's faults.

To be merciful as God is merciful creates a happy state. It joins us

Until those of us who call ourselves Christians repent and move beyond exclusions that we have tolerated, justified, or perpetuated, we cannot with integrity call ourselves the messengers of the Lord's loving-kindness.

—Helen Bruch Pearson

to all humanity so we need not carry the burden of imagined superiority. It makes us mindful of how easily faults can overtake us, the subtlety of the webs of deceit and temptation, and our inadequate knowledge about the inner struggles of others to live rightly.

Robert Morris relates the struggle he had dealing with his aged father after his mother's death. His father was "a highly responsible man afflicted by high anxiety, a violent temper, and a critical, demeaning tongue." Reluctantly and slowly, but in obedience to Christ's command to love, Robert began to pray for his father and to offer a type of professional empathy. He started to gain insight into the fear and pain behind his father's behavior. Beneath long-held anger, Robert discovered his own frustrated love. "Gradually, over a period of years," he wrote, "merciful kindness began to dawn. I began to see the heroic battle my dad actually had fought to keep his temper and violent actions under restraint."[4] Finally, Robert had a vivid dream about his father as a young man, from which he awoke knowing that mercy had triumphed over wrath in his own heart. He felt free from the prison of his resentment. He had embraced the wisdom of tenderness and discovered the happiness of the merciful.

The reward of being merciful and the promise of receiving mercy is not an "I scratch your back, you scratch mine" proposition or a quid pro quo "spiritual bargain." The beatitude expresses a deep inner principle of connection, the same connection behind Jesus' words, "Forgive, and you will be forgiven; give, and it will be given to you" (Luke 6:37-38). If we want friends, we need to be a friend. If we would have mercy, we must show mercy. Our mercy toward others shows that we are ready to receive the mercy God offers us. We might express the dynamic this way:

> Take the trouble of [others] to your heart, and in the day of your trouble you shall reap, in the love of other hearts, the harvest of your heart's unselfish sowing.[5]

God's concern and, by extension, our concern, is to be directed toward those who are last and least.

—Wendy M. Wright

The Sowing of Mercy

The work of mercy waits for us in an infinite variety of forms, emerging from the ever-changing stream of life. Each expression is rooted in the posture of humility and outgoing love. In addition to refraining from judgment, we can refrain from taking pleasure in the losses, shortcomings, or misfortunes of others. This common and secret form of mercilessness breeds in the swamp of jealousy, satisfying our desire to feel superior. It is jarring to discover it in our hearts.

Beyond refraining from judgment and jealousy, mercy takes many active forms. In his delightful paraphrase of the Rule of Benedict, John McQuiston lists these expressions of "right relationship":

> to relieve the unhappy,
> to visit the sick,
> to clothe the destitute,
> to shelter the oppressed, …
> to support the troubled,
> to encourage good humor,
> to forgive our enemies,
> to show mercy to the weak.[6]

Those willing to enter into the painful places of life with others will find the true happiness of mercy. A children's cancer ward is not a place many of us would choose to visit unless we felt obliged to by kinship or friendship. Some of us might imagine we could not bear to see the fragile bodies of dying children or the desperate eyes of their parents. But the reward of those who visit as a service of mercy is often incalculable. The words shared, the gestures offered, the responses received can bring lasting joy in the midst of grief to both caregivers and care-receivers.[7]

Mercy gives us sympathy for the plight of every human life. When we know our own need of God's mercy with utter conviction, we can empathize freely with people of all characters and conditions. W. Paul Jones writes compellingly of his visits to a condemned man on death row. The humanity of this man accused of murder emerges more

[The merciful are] those who have an attitude of such compassion toward all people that they want to share gladly all that they have with one another and with the world.

—Clarence Jordan

*The quality of mercy is not strain'd,
It droppeth as the gentle rain from heaven
Upon the place beneath: it is twice blest;
It blesseth him that gives, and him that takes.*

—William Shakespeare

clearly with each visit. His desire for redemption is poignant. Who is beyond God's mercy? Who is beyond ours?

Building on the foundation of humility and hunger for God's just reign, we move from gentle heartedness to generous heartedness, from meekness to mercy. Mercy is a natural outgrowth of righteousness—that "inward, vital, joyous righteousness rooted in true love of God and humanity."[8] Such outgoing love and tenderness serve as direct expressions of kingdom life. If we hoard God's mercy for ourselves, it vanishes like uneaten manna. "The one condition of ownership is that it be given away."[9] In the giving we ourselves are deeply nourished, and our hunger for God's life in communion with others is satisfied.

Here, then, is the paradox of this beatitude: In the economy of God's realm, what we give away is not depleted but multiplied. Kingdom mathematics is based on addition and multiplication, not subtraction or division. When Peter tried to get his arithmetic straight on forgiveness, Jesus gave him an answer he probably couldn't calculate (70 x 7, RSV). God doesn't calculate in giving to us, and we are not to calculate either but to give with joyful abandon. Mercy comes from the abundance of God's heart—abundance of pardon, grace, healing, life, joy! Thomas Merton described the mystery well when he said that God's heart is "Mercy within mercy within mercy."[10] Such is the depth of wisdom in tenderness. Happy indeed are those who know and share the gift!

DAILY EXERCISES

Throughout this week, be especially aware of the many acts of mercy you see. Begin by reading Week Six, "Embracing the Wisdom of Tenderness," and recording your thoughts in your journal. The daily exercises challenge us to live in grateful awareness of God's generous mercy toward us. As you reflect on each of the daily exercises, let your awareness of the abundance of God's mercy open you to a more generous heart toward others. Prepare yourself for your daily time of reflection by coming humbly before God in thanksgiving.

EXERCISE 1   LISTENING TO JESUS

Read Matthew 4:23–5:7. Make a list of "the merciful" in your life. Lift them to God as they come to mind and bless them. Beside each name, jot down memories of ways that each showed mercy toward you or served as a model for being merciful. In what sense do you think they will "receive mercy"?

Say the beatitude aloud several times. Reflect on what it means to you and put your thoughts together in the form of one or more paraphrases.

Open your heart to the gift of God's mercy. Pray that you may grow to be merciful as God is merciful (see Luke 6:36). Be honest with God about the parts of you that may not want that gift. Nonetheless, rest in God's mercy.

EXERCISE 2   THINKING OF GOD'S MERCIES

Read Psalm 103:1-5 and Romans 12:1-2. "Bless the Lord...and do not forget all his benefits" by pausing to savor each verse and recalling ways you have experienced the mercy that the verse names. After verses 1-5, add your own verses to express specific ways you have experienced God's mercy at work (such as, "who gives me breath for another day," "who heals my marriage," "who reconciles us when we are bitterly divided"). Write these "verses" in your journal.

The Jerusalem Bible translates Romans 12:1, "Think of God's mercy...and worship...in a way that is worthy of thinking beings, by offering your living bodies as a holy sacrifice." How does thinking about God's mercy in Jesus Christ and God's mercies in your life mold your mind-set and influence your behavior? What divine invitation or prompting do you hear?

Share your gratitude with God for all God's benefits. Acknowledge any invitation you may hear. Pray for the full gift of God's mercy in your life.

EXERCISE 3   FILLING YOUR LOVE BUCKET

Read Luke 7:36-50. In this story, Jesus suggests that being forgiven much leads to loving much; being forgiven little leads to loving little. Put yourself in the place of the "woman…who was a sinner." Soak in the gift of God's "great love" and acceptance that you receive in Jesus' presence. In response, imagine yourself standing behind Jesus and bathing his feet with the tears of your gratitude and the oil of your love. When he turns, whose face of human need does he wear? Continue to bathe whomever you see in prayer.

Take a moment to consider the source and supply of love in your life. Draw a big bucket and fill it with symbols of love, acceptance, and forgiveness that you have received and that continue to flow in your direction. Top it off with the great love of God in Jesus Christ that is yours through the Spirit. Close your eyes and open your heart to the constant flow of God's love for your filling and outpouring. As you interact with people, carry within you this prayer image of an overflowing, self-replenishing supply of divine mercy that wants to be shared and from which you can freely draw. Record your experience in your journal.

EXERCISE 4   OVERCOMING OBSTACLES TO MERCY

Read Luke 13:10-17. This is one of numerous stories in which Jesus offered mercy where mercy was otherwise denied or obstructed. Enter imaginatively into this woman's situation. Try to visualize what she would see and feel on a daily basis. Ponder what could have bent her over or given her a crippling spirit. Observe the obstacles to her even being noticed, much less receiving help from God or people. Contemplate the mercy Jesus showed with several simple actions. List the action words.

Who in your life is bent over or weighed down by circumstances, afflicted by a crippling spirit, or denied mercy? What obstacles to mercy are at work in each situation? Reflect on how Jesus' care might flow out of you toward this person. Ponder the little actions that could make a world of difference and overcome the obstacles to mercy.

Hold those who come to mind in prayer. Imagine what Jesus would do and could do through you. Record your thoughts.

EXERCISE 5   CLOTHING YOURSELF IN THE MERCIES OF CHRIST DAILY

Read Colossians 3:12-15. To "clothe yourself with compassion, kindness, humility, meekness, and patience" is a spiritual discipline. Read the passage again slowly. List all the kinds of Christ-clothing that these verses name. Imagine clothing yourself with each aspect of Christ. As you do so, note what old "clothes" need to come off.

As an act of daily prayer, try clothing yourself with Christ as you dress. As a way of remaining clothed in Christ, commit a verse of this passage to memory and carry it in you. Reflect on how such a practice influences your daily interactions. Record your experience.

Remember to review the insights recorded in your notebook or journal for the week in preparation for the group meeting.

Week 7

Receiving the Vision of God

> *"Blessed are the pure in heart,*
> *for they will see God."*

This is perhaps the most mysterious and beautiful of all the beatitudes. Surely it contains the most attractive promise conceivable, to see the glory and vitality of the Source of all life! But the meaning of these words is not self-evident. They invite deep reflection. What exactly is "purity of heart"? And how can we "see God"?

A Pure Heart: Clearing the Wellspring Within

I had an experience recently that revealed my heart to me in a way I would have preferred not to see. I was negotiating with a man to do some home repairs in preparation for our upcoming move. He came highly recommended for quality workmanship. I wanted to pay him by check or to receive from him a cash receipt. He wanted cash with no receipt, that being the way he had always done business. The more I tried ever so reasonably to explain why he needed to accept one of my two payment options, the more he dug his heels in. Stubborn resistance met every angle of persuasion or argument I could muster.

The point I wish to make has little to do with the merit of my case. What got my attention was my reaction. Waves of heat and irritation rose up inside me, along with my heart and pulse rate. My "fight" response marshaled all my intellect, feeling, and will to convince this man that he should choose one of the paths I presented. Even

as we spoke, I realized that my response was not what I wished it to be. However calm and rational I may have sounded as we conversed, I had no gentle spirit of clarity or peace within. Ending the conversation feeling drained and defeated, I understood that my heart had just been revealed to me.

The ancients did not mean mere emotion when they spoke of the heart. We think of heart primarily as feeling and sentiment. But in biblical times, heart represented the sum of a person's interior life, especially the mind and will. With the heart as "the source of all our reactions and aspirations,"[1] both good and evil can spring from it. So the sense of this beatitude is "blessed are those who have a pure source of life in them."[2]

Think for a moment about the meanings associated with purity. It can mean clean, as in pure water; it can mean a single substance, as in pure gold; it can mean only, as in a pure liquid diet. In moral terms it can mean faultless or unstained. Purity also has connotations of integrity, honesty, and unity. In Psalm 24, those who may "ascend the hill of the LORD" have "clean hands and pure hearts," meaning that they resist falsehood (Ps. 24:3-4). A pure heart is one without the "alloy" of deceit or double mindedness. It is single, unified in its intent toward God. The great Christian philosopher Søren Kierkegaard believed that "purity of heart is to will one thing."

Purity gathers up the previous beatitudes and is a wonderful word if not narrowed to mere morality. "It is not a virtue, it is all the virtues."[3] We come to purity through each beatitude—humbly acknowledging our utter need for God; mourning our fallen, faulty state; moving meekly, with gentle but clear intent through this world; hungering more and more for God's rightly ordered reign; growing in willing and impartial mercy for all. This is the pathway to purity of heart.

So what is the state of our heart? How clear is the source of life within us? God has placed in us a likeness to the divine being; we are meant to reflect God's image the way clear waters reflect what is above them. But in our need to determine our own lives, we have muddied the waters. We tend to settle for external expressions of purity that don't get to the heart of things.

External forms of piety or purity never impressed Jesus. All the washing of hands and pots and pans so dear to the Pharisees was of little importance to him (see Mark 7:2-4). The Jews of his day had great concern about what defiled a person. Jesus said, "It is what comes out of a person that defiles. For it is from within, from the human heart, that evil intentions come" (Mark 7:20-21). God's interest lies in the motives and intentions beneath outward forms. Indeed, God sees the heart with perfect clarity.

Consider this simple test of your heart. Ask yourself the following questions:

- How do I think or react when something happens unexpectedly?
- When a person crosses me or speaks an unkind word, what comes spontaneously from within me?
- When a person compliments or praises me, what is my immediate and instinctive reaction?

Simplicity can help us focus on the one treasure of great value, our relationship with God.

—Ann Hagmann

Your reactions at these moments can be quite revealing. They show your inner orientation to life, the habits of thought and will that govern you. Observing your responses to sudden situations can be a helpful exercise in self-awareness, just as I became conscious of my inward response to the home repairman.

Thankfully, our unhelpful spontaneous responses can be transformed. God desires to give us a clean heart, to put "a new and right spirit" within us (Ps. 51:10). In John's Gospel Jesus quotes scripture saying, "Out of the believer's heart shall flow rivers of living water" (7:37-38). He was referring to the Spirit that believers would receive, a source of pure water welling up from within to replace the muddied waters of our heart. As the mud clears, the heart begins to "see" again.

Seeing God and Seeing as God Sees

When it comes to seeing God, the Bible offers more paradox. No one can see the face of God and live, yet Moses spoke with God "face to face" (Exod. 33:11). God is invisible, yet Jesus is "the image of the invisible God" (Col.1:15). Jesus even says to Philip, "Whoever has seen me has seen the Father" (John 14:9). Like purity, the word *seeing* has more than one meaning. In addition to physical sight, we speak of understanding, perception, insight, and vision as metaphors for spiritual or intellectual sight. We can indeed "see God" in metaphorical ways, while never exhausting the divine mystery.

The vision of God is a promise held out to all, not just to mystics and prophets. Moreover it is intended for this world, not only the world to come. Yes, the fullness of vision remains for a future yet to be revealed: "For now we see in a mirror, dimly, but then we will see face to face" (1 Cor. 13:12). Yet in the meantime, "faith, hope, and love abide," the very qualities that enable us to "see God" here and now. Faith, hope, and love are expressions of a pure heart. They help us to perceive the nearness of God's realm and help to bring it near. This beatitude embodies a profound truth: As we are, so we see.

> *The impure shall see all—except God. That is to say, they shall see nothing as it is.*
>
> —Percy C. Ainsworth

We know that our inner state often determines how we view life. When we are "down," we see everything as dark and heavy no matter how bright the day or how cheery our companions. When we are happy, we see optimistically regardless of how dreary the day or how cynical our friends. If changing moods so dramatically affect our seeing, how much more with abiding tempers of the heart! If filled with suspicion, we will view people and events as suspicious. But if we are full of love, we will find evidence of love everywhere.

What happens if we discover a wellspring of life within that is God's own life, pure and fresh? Surely this is the discovery of the apostle Paul when he said, "It is no longer I who live, but it is Christ who lives in me" (Gal. 2:20). If faith, hope, and love have become the abiding habits of our hearts, then we know the indwelling of God. With eyes unclouded by self-regard, we begin to see God all around us and to see as God sees.

To see things as they truly are is to see as God sees. God sees goodness, light, eternal joy. God sees creation as intended and willed in God's own heart. Perhaps for this reason the prophet Habakkuk says of God, "Your eyes are too pure to behold evil" (1:13), and why Titus says, "To the pure all things are pure" (Titus 1:15). One writer puts it this way: "To have a pure heart means that wherever you look, whatever you are looking at, what you see is God."[4]

Seeing God in all things means seeing the imprint of God in all that is made. Anthony the Great once responded to a scholar who asked how he could be so happy while deprived of good books: "My book, O philosopher, is the nature of created things, and any time I want to read the words of God, the book is before me."[5] The Christian mystic Meister Eckhart likewise encouraged his readers to perceive God in all things: "Every single creature is full of God and is a book about God."[6] Where do you see God in the created order?

To see God in all things includes perceiving the divine presence in every human being and all human situations. If the tiniest caterpillar is a "book about God," how many more volumes is a human being created in the very image and likeness of God! The great reformer Martin Luther wisely noted:

> There are those who seek to penetrate the immensities and to see God. One ought rather to sink into the depths and seek to find God among the suffering and the downtrodden. Then the heart is free from pride and able to see God.[7]

Where do you see God in the faces of those around you? Can you see Christ in the eyes of the needy, the disabled, even the mean-spirited? However obscured by pain, disfigurement, or sin, the image of God is still present. Have we enough love to see?

To notice God in everyday "epiphanies" of nature and human life is to see as an artist or poet sees, looking beyond the surface and penetrating to the meaning, which cannot be found apart from divine presence and purpose. Grace is simply God's real presence with us, "the active goodness of God in our lives."[8] Where do we perceive grace in the midst of each day? To see divine presence shining through the ordinary is to cultivate heartfelt wonder.

You may be asking, What about evil? Can we possibly see God in the face of evil? One spiritual writer I have found especially helpful in this area suggests that a person restored to purity of heart is not afraid to look anything in the face—neither the attraction of beauty nor

We need to let ourselves be "tempted" by a sense of God's immanence, a sense that sees God everywhere, God in things, God in nature, God "in every place."
—Carlo Caretto

the ugliness of sin.[9] As purity of heart clarifies our vision, we begin to see human beings as good even if their choices are evil. We notice that evil results from a distortion of something essentially good. For example, sexual addictions sometimes express a misguided desire for love. Harsh discipline is often a misguided effort to be responsible. The need to control others may grow from a strong desire to bring order out of chaos. No one is totally devoid of goodness or humanity.

Moreover, in the economy of God's will for this world, God can use even our sin as "all things work together for good" (Rom. 8:28). Evil is not an independent power equal to God in this universe. "It is a mystery,...which somehow arises as a weakness within the good."[10] The cross of Christ exemplifies God's desire and power to turn the worst evil into the greatest good. A pure heart enables us to see God's redemptive suffering in all kinds of evil. "To have a pure heart is.... to have a heart like the heart of Christ, taking into itself all the anger and hatred of [human beings] and consuming them in and into a fire of infinite love."[11] What a hope for genuine transformation!

Finally we return to the essence of all the beatitudes. The ultimate blessedness is to be like God, full of humble love as God is humble in immense love toward us. We are to mourn our broken covenant and the death it introduces into this beautiful world as God mourns our spiritual sickness and death. We are to be as gentle hearted as Christ, as merciful as our heavenly Father, hungry for a righteousness like God's, and pure in heart as God is. This is our supreme happiness and bliss in life: to be like God.

The vision of God is for all who open their hearts and submit to the grace of the Holy Spirit. The Spirit slowly changes our hearts from stone into flesh (Ezek. 36:26). With this transformation we begin to see God and to see as God sees. None of us is wholly pure, however great our faith or love. Yet "He who laid His hands...on sightless eyes is waiting to lay that healing touch on your sightless heart."[12] May we come to the wisdom of the poet in that rich hymn lyric,

> Heart of my own heart, whatever befall,
> Still be my vision, O Ruler of all.[13]

Purity of heart clarifies things,...so that we can see even sin in the context of a whole vision of God and of [God's] providence.

—Simon Tugwell

DAILY EXERCISES

Read and reflect on Week Six, "Receiving the Vision of God." Jesus' teaching on the Great Commandment (Matt 22:37) clearly calls, not merely for the avoidance of impure thoughts, but for the single-minded and whole-hearted devotion appropriate to faith in one God. Each daily exercise offers the opportunity for you to give your heart fully to God. Prepare yourself for each time of reflection by taking a few moments to clear your head of distractions and invite God's direction. EXERCISE 5 will serve as preparation for the Deeper Explorations in the next meeting.

EXERCISE 1   LISTENING TO JESUS

Read Matthew 5:1-8. Focus first on what it means to "see God." Locate and write where you are able to "see God" in life and in the world. Also locate and write where you are least able to "see God" in the world. In each case, what are you looking for? What does it mean to you to "see God"?

Shift your focus to "pure in heart." Recall the line in the week's reading that says, "We know that our inner state often determines how we view life." Now reflect on the relationship between where you can and cannot "see God" and the state of your inner life.

Paraphrase in your own words what you think Jesus was really blessing and calling forth in this beatitude.

Spend a few minutes in prayer with the beatitude. As people come to mind, lift them to God and bless them. Ask God to help you see what blurs your vision of God in them. Record your insights and experiences.

EXERCISE 2   CULTIVATING AN EYE FOR GOD

Read Matthew 6:22-23. Draw a picture of how you see your life when "your eye is healthy." Draw a second picture of how you see your life when "your eye is unhealthy." What do the pictures reveal to you about yourself?

Conclude with a time for cultivating a single eye by practicing a

So then, the things we miss seeing are the things we miss being.
—Percy C. Ainsworth

form of Centering Prayer. Choose a single centering word or phrase, such as *God, pure, see, blessed,* or *heart.* For several minutes repeat the word prayerfully and leisurely in sync with the rhythm of your breathing. Open a space for God within you, setting aside other thoughts and worries that compete for your attention.

Write about your experience. How does it affect what you see? Continue to take time to practice this kind of Centering Prayer.

EXERCISE 3   STRIVING FIRST FOR THE KINGDOM

Read Matthew 6:24-33. Purity of heart is "undivided" (Ps. 86:11) in its striving "first for the kingdom of God and his righteousness." Draw a circle. At the center of the circle, write what you "strive first for." Out from the center, identify what "all these things" are for you, that is, the other things to which you commit real time and energy. What about this picture are you at peace with and not at peace with?

Conclude by practicing your Centering Prayer for a few minutes. Or pray using a word or phrase from this passage. Carry your Centering Prayer throughout the day and notice how it affects your perspective on what's central. Record your learning.

EXERCISE 4   BEING TRANSPARENT TO CHRIST

Read Acts 5:1-11. Some of the earliest reports of the New Testament church describe it as a pure reflection of the life of Christ in community. Acts 4:32-34 celebrates how the community was "of one heart and soul" and "there was not a needy person among them." Yet Acts 5:1-11 tells how spiritual death came to the community when two members lied to God and chose to live double lives, spiritually speaking.

Reflect in your journal on your church: (a) In what ways do you see your church reflecting the heart and holiness of the living Christ in its common life and ministry? (b) In what ways do you think your transparency to Christ is clouded? Name the clouds.

In prayer, seek God's face about how you and your church can restore your transparency to Christ. Write what you see or hear in your journal.

[Those who] live a double life spiritually ...are anything but blessed. Their conflicting loyalties make them wretched, confused, tense. And having to keep their eyes on two masters at once makes them cross-eyed.

—Clarence Jordan

EXERCISE 5   SEEING YOUR COMPANIONS IN CHRIST

Read 2 Corinthians 5:15-17. Not only does Paul no longer judge Christ by worldly standards; he no longer regards anyone from a human point of view. "See, everything has become new" for those who are in Christ.

Practice this new way of seeing. Write the name of a person you know well, friend or foe. First, describe how you see him or her from a human point of view, that is, in terms of your likes and dislikes, needs and prejudices. Second, describe how Christ sees them, that is, the One "who died and was raised for them."

Now take a few moments to contemplate each member of your *Companions* group. Lift each person to God, one by one, and see each individual for who he or she is to Christ and in Christ. Beside each name, write a phrase or sentence that reflects the blessing you see and celebrate in that person.

Remember to review the insights recorded in your notebook or journal for the week in preparation for the group meeting.

Week 8
Making Peace,
an Offering of Love

"Blessed are the peacemakers,
for they will be called children of God."

*I*f we were to look at news headlines from the past several years, they would include banners like these: "Peacekeeper Mission in Bosnia Begins," "Mid-East Peace Talks on Hold," "Longest Peace Time Economy in History."

The world thinks of peace as the absence of war. Although rudimentary, this understanding is not a bad place to begin. War, the most destructive and horrifying sign of fractured peace in human life, makes visible the devastation of human sin. In the two-hundred-year nationhood of the United States, we have been at war at least ten times: the Revolutionary War, the War of 1812, the Civil War, the Spanish-American War, World War I, World War II, the Korean conflict, the Vietnam War, the Gulf War, and the Iraqi War. No generation of Americans has been untouched by the suffering and loss that accompanied at least one war, either on our soil or abroad.

What the world calls peace and what God's Word calls peace reflect different orders of reality. The connections between the two orders are best seen through the lens of faith rather than the media of the world.

The Peace of God

Peace is not simply the absence of war or the absence of less evident conflict. Sometimes we do not see underlying conflict because it has

been suppressed. For example, European colonialism suppressed tribal conflicts in various parts of Africa for a time, just as ironfisted dictators suppressed ethnic conflicts in the Balkans. Predictably, when the controls were removed these conflicts erupted with vicious force. Powerful countries often try to "keep the peace" in countries where they have vested economic or political interests. When most governments speak of peace, they talk about stability and national security. But enforced "peace," especially without justice, can become a breeding ground for future conflict.

Peace is...something which enfolds us rather than something which we grasp.
—Simon Tugwell

The prophet Jeremiah understood what people in powerful positions meant by the language of peace. Pointing out that even the priests and prophets of Israel dealt in falsehood and greed for gain, he laments: "They have treated the wound of my people carelessly, saying, 'Peace, peace,' when there is no peace" (6:14).

The biblical vision of peace is much richer and more far-reaching than that of the world. Hebrew and Christian scriptures ascribe many meanings to *peace*: "rest, ease, security, completeness, shalom, quietness, and unity."[1] Peace may be held within, given to others, taken back, made, or followed. The word most commonly translated "peace" in the Hebrew Scriptures is *shalom*, the holistic well-being of persons in a faithful community. Shalom, the daily blessing of God's peace that Jews bestowed upon one another long before Jesus' time, is a lively tradition to this day in the Jewish community. Shalom connotes healing, wholeness, righteousness, unity, harmony, and total contentment. The mending wholeness of shalom is an apt image of salvation, the one eternal purpose God clearly wills for the world.

Jesus came to proclaim, embody, and promise the fullness of God's peace. As the Prince of Peace, Christ shows us a kingdom in which no cause for strife can exist. The kingdom of heaven is the reign of perfect love, and those who belong to this kingdom are governed by love as an inner guiding principle. Writing from prison to the Colossian church, Paul understands the connection between holy love and peace: "Above all, clothe yourselves with love.... And let the peace of Christ rule in your hearts" (Col. 3:14-15).

Receiving God's Peace

From experience we discover that unless peace emerges from within us it cannot take root beyond us. We cannot manufacture peace in our families, neighborhoods, or world by sheer good intentions and hard work. Like all good things, peace comes to us first as gift. As we ourselves are ministered to by God's mercy and peace, we in turn are able to minister the grace and peace of God to others.

We receive this peace first by accepting God's sacrificial gift in the reconciling grace of Christ. "Sin is the one and only disturber of the peace."[2] Sin breaks the infinitely just and tender law of love that constitutes the life of the human soul and the bond of community under the reign of God. Since the great enemy of peace is sin, God provides a solution to our deadly conflicts that goes right to their core. The solution comes at a terrible price. The feet of the messenger of peace are wounded feet. Yet God, in Christ, willingly pays the price because of the immensity of divine love. "For in him all the fullness of God was pleased to dwell, and through him God was pleased to reconcile to himself all things, whether on earth or in heaven, by making peace through the blood of his cross" (Col. 1:19-20).

The letter to the Ephesians, addressing Gentiles and Jews who had been locked in mortal enmity for generations, powerfully expresses the relationship of the cross to human peace:

> But now in Christ Jesus you who once were far off have been brought near by the blood of Christ. For he is our peace; in his flesh he has made both groups into one and has broken down the dividing wall, that is, the hostility between us…. So he came and proclaimed peace to you who were far off and peace to those who were near; for through him both of us have access in one Spirit to the Father. (2:13-14, 17-18)

The cross makes clear that the governing principle of God's kingdom is self-giving love, "a fragrant offering and sacrifice to God" (Eph. 5:2). Self-giving love is the principle of Jesus' life and death; he offers this love to us, for he gives us himself. "He is our peace," embodying

The consuming desire of God seems to have been voiced by the angels at the birth of [God's] Son: "…on earth, peace!"

—Clarence Jordan

all that makes for peace. If we live in union with him, we have "the peace of God, which surpasses all understanding," the great gift he would leave with us (John 14:27). We move from accepting the gift of Christ to living in Christ, absorbing his reconciling grace and allowing it to transform us into peaceful and peacemaking followers.

Every beatitude provides a stepping-stone to life in Christ, enabling us to be makers of peace. Indeed, each beatitude carries its own quality of divine peace:

- In poverty of spirit we acknowledge our inability to create for ourselves the abundant life that only God can give. The open-handed need of our poverty is a peaceful posture, like that of a trusting child.

- Lamenting our brokenness and mourning our losses, we are carried to the only lasting source of hope and peace: the great, divine Lover's embrace.

- The self-respecting gentleness of the meek shows the peace of clarity and rest; the gentle need not expend energy proving or defending themselves. Their powers are yielded peaceably to God's will.

- Hunger and thirst for righteousness provide the building blocks for peace, since true peace comes only with the just order of God's reign.

- Unless zeal for righteousness resides in the spaciousness of mercy, it cannot bring the peace of God. God's forgiving mercy brings us peace of conscience, as our mercy brings such peace to others.

- Purity of heart is inseparable from peace, for there can be no peace where our hearts are inwardly divided. Peace of heart comes with unity of vision.

To live the beatitudes as a whole is to become a true child of God. To be a child of the God of peace is to be a peacemaker. The chief characteristics of the Parent are recognized in the child, and the child reflects the divine Parent's "spiritual genes." Ponder this insight: Peace-

> *The peaceful—and therefore the peace-making—life is the life lived in harmony with the divine order.*
>
> —Percy C. Ainsworth

makers are children of God not because they make peace; rather they make peace because they live with integrity as children of God, prepared to do God's will.

The Work of Peace

As children of God we become heirs with Christ to all the riches of the kingdom, "naturalized citizens" of our true home. We become part of the new creation, from which the work of peace flows naturally and graciously in the freedom of the heart. This infinitely adaptable work wells up spontaneously under the active guidance of the Holy Spirit. The Spirit will adapt to circumstances as well as to our unique gifts and sense of call.

Peace does not seek strife or a quarrel in any way, but always seeks gentleness.
—Hildegard of Bingen

Among the early followers of Jesus, the way of peace meant not taking up arms or defending themselves. For the first three hundred years of their history, Christians lived out a deep commitment to nonviolence, clearly understood to be the way of Christ. Jesus never took up arms or formed an army; he refused to defend himself when arrested and taken to trial. He was meek in the highest sense, and his early disciples followed his way. It is a path worthy of deep consideration in our time, when so much of Jesus' way among us has been diluted or compromised by the world's values. Nonviolent resistance to evil, a key expression of the work of peace, is the more dramatic and visibly noble side of peacemaking.

In everyday situations we go about the work of peace by demonstrating calmness, simplicity, patience, and courtesy. When have you experienced workdays of intense competition, anxiety, and pressure to accomplish? Embodying a different kind of presence in such a day invites your coworkers to see tasks and events from a new perspective. Do the monotonous routines of home life bore you, or do the irritating habits of those you live with chafe at you? We may do some of the best work of peace in the relative anonymity of family life, where the disciplines of gentleness, clarity, and forgiving love can mend fatigued, fussy, and foul tempers in our intimate relationships.

Peacemaking may come in the hidden service of deep listening, holy silence, and gracious speech. Rachel Pinney, a doctor and anti-nuclear activist, learned that the more she tried to convince people of her views, the more they resisted her message. She decided to try listening instead of speaking, actively seeking out people who disagreed with her. She did nothing but listen to their views and periodically reflect to them what she had heard so they could correct any inaccuracies. Pinney discovered that when people did not feel pressured to defend their views, they could step back and gain perspective on what they had said. Some even began to reexamine their ideas for the first time, simply because her deep listening allowed them to begin to hear themselves clearly.[3]

Making peace can come through simple generosity of spirit and persevering acts of kindness, as in the "one by one" strategy of love that sustained Mother Teresa of Calcutta who took her professed name from Thérèse of Lisieux. At one point, Thérèse chose to show special daily kindness to an old, disagreeable sister in the convent whom no one else could bear. Thérèse summoned extra energy each day to stop the old sister and offer a pleasant word, a smile, flowers, or whatever she "would do for the person I loved the most." Gradually the unhappy woman's personality began to lighten and change. The peace of reconciliation started to take hold in Thérèse's community. God's love works to transform the neediest and least attractive among us, if we willingly collaborate with grace. Once again we see the integral connection between mercy and peace.

There is another face to making peace, however. "The peacemaker has sometimes to appear to be a peace-breaker."[4] God's own justice and freedom form the ground of true peace. Only with genuine effort are authentic justice and freedom gained and preserved. The world may give lip service to these kingdom values while in reality dismiss them because they threaten to reveal its own cherished values of domination and control. Accomplishing the work of peace requires the exposure of our idols and comforting illusions.

"The peace which Christ gives to us is 'no peace by the world's standards.'"[5] Jesus himself says he comes not to bring peace but a

We should be peaceful in words and deeds and in our way of life.
—Angela of Foligno

sword (Matt. 10:34). Other passages in scripture speak figuratively of the sword as an image of the Spirit (Eph. 6:17) and of God's finely discerning word (Heb. 4:12). Jesus seems to be teaching us to value the way of God's word and spirit above all else. This valuing may involve a price that divides us from those who do not understand or desire the reign of God. Yet Jesus assures us that we will find our true selves precisely as we lose our worldly selves.

We have much to relinquish in order to gain God's peace: the idols of our security—possessions, power, defenses; the dynamics that control us—consumerism, competition, fear, and greed. These must be repudiated. They are death to the soul. We should be prepared for our own resistance to such uprooting. The dominating powers of this world and the proud or wounded ego in us that consciously or unconsciously cooperates with them will object mightily. But only by uprooting can we move forward on the path to renewed health, and thus to our deepest blessedness and joy.

Our surrender to the humility, gentleness, righteousness, mercy, and purity of God is the greatest power under heaven, holding our promise of transformation and our highest joy. The promise foretold by Zechariah at the birth of his son, John, still shines before us:

> By the tender mercy of our God,
>   the dawn from on high will break upon us,
> to give light to those who sit in darkness and in the shadow of death,
>   to guide our feet into the way of peace. (Luke 1:78-79)

DAILY EXERCISES

Read and reflect on Week Eight, "Making Peace: A Fragrant Offering of Love." As you work through the exercises, consider the contribution of all the beatitudes to your capacity to be a peacemaker. Let each of the daily exercises be an opportunity to listen to God's call, and give yourself more fully to your vocation as a disciple of Jesus Christ: helping people make peace with God and one another.

EXERCISE 1   LISTENING TO JESUS

Read Matthew 5:9. The word *peacemaker*, a term unique to the Gospel of Matthew, can mean different things. What do you think or hope Jesus intended to bless? What do you assume or hope he did not bless?

Consider the fact that Roman emperors also called themselves "peacemakers" and "sons of God" in Jesus' day. What contrasts does Jesus highlight between the peace God makes and the peace Rome makes, between living in God's likeness or in Caesar's likeness?

Reflect on this beatitude as the fruit of the beatitudes as a whole, a summary image for the blessing and calling of Christian disciples. Viewed in that light, what does this beatitude say to you about the nature of your true vocation and growth as a follower of Jesus?

Note your reflections; write your paraphrase of this beatitude.

EXERCISE 2   THE CHALLENGE OF SHALOM

Read Micah 4:1-4. This is one of several Old Testament prophecies of shalom (lasting peace, wholeness, and well-being) for the Hebrew people and for the world. As you meditate on this passage, identify and jot down some of the key features of shalom alluded to here.

Select a few verses for deeper meditation, following the suggestions below:

Verse 2 calls us to "Come." Where can "peoples" and "nations" go today "that [the Lord] may teach us his ways and that we may walk in his paths"? If you wanted to learn the art of peacemaking, where would you go and what would you expect to learn?

Verse 3 says the Lord will "arbitrate." Imagine the designated leaders of two nations in serious conflict meeting with the Lord for arbitration. Choose the nations and imagine the scene. What case would each plead to justify its position? Listen to the Lord's response to each. Write out what the Lord might tell the leaders and the nations they will need to learn and do before they will enjoy God's shalom.

Verse 3 also says nations will convert their means of war into means of peace. Use your own prophetic imagination to visualize what would be involved and who would be affected by such a complete conversion of materials, mind-sets, and human resources. What do you see happening? How would it affect you? How does this kind of dreaming make you feel?

Verse 4 says people will no longer have to be afraid of one another. Who generates fear in you? In whom do you generate fear? Identify one action you could take to diminish your fear or someone else's fear of you.

Be still and sit with God in peace. Ask the Lord to show you where and how you can remove obstacles to shalom.

EXERCISE 3   PASSING THE PEACE HOUSE TO HOUSE

Read Luke 10:1-12. Jesus sent the seventy on a mission of peace, instructing them to say, "Peace to this house" before entering any home and to make the kingdom of God a reality wherever the people welcomed them. Reflect on the wisdom in Jesus' instructions for apostles as peacemakers. Which ones can you translate into instructions for today?

Imagine Jesus sending you and your group in pairs to visit homes and families in your neighborhood as ambassadors of God's peace. What instructions and help might he offer for passing the peace? Record your reflections.

Go to God in prayer for peace. Seek God's guidance as to the best way to go about building peace where you live.

EXERCISE 4   STAYING AT THE TABLE

Read Mark 14:17-25. At the Last Supper, Jesus preserves the peace by staying at the table with his disciples, even though he knows that "one of you will betray me" and all would desert him. Meditate on the sacrificial character of Jesus' action in this dramatic picture of the peace that God's love makes possible. When have you seen someone "stay at the table" for the sake of preserving the bond of peace despite others' actions? When have you been the one to make the sacrifice?

Select one place in your life where you know the fellowship to be broken. Visualize ways in which peace might be restored. Imagine everyone gathered at a common table with Jesus. What would Jesus ask of you? What would he give you? What are you willing to give him for the sake of the fellowship?

Spend a few moments prayerfully listening for what is called for on your part to be a peacemaker. Note your insights.

EXERCISE 5   PURSUING WHAT MAKES FOR PEACE

Read Romans 14:13-23. Paul challenges the Christians in Rome to use their freedom to "pursue what makes for peace and for mutual upbuilding," not to exercise their freedom in a manner that puts "a stumbling block…in the way of another." Yet any newspaper will pinpoint two or more places where people are fighting over conflicting rights to exercise their freedom as they please. Where do you experience the same conflict in the church or community?

Apply Paul's high standard to a situation you know. How would that situation be affected if one or both of the parties agreed to "pursue what makes for peace" above particular interests? How might you pursue creative resolution through "mutual upbuilding" rather than adversarial methods that result in winners and losers?

Identify an issue and conviction about which you are passionate. Bring to mind those who hold an opposing view. Go together, in your mind, before the cross of Christ. Open yourself to the gift and challenge that Christ wants to give you from the cross.

Remember to review the insights recorded in your notebook or journal for the week in preparation for the group meeting.

Week 9
The Deep Gladness of Suffering Love

"Blessed are those who are persecuted for righteousness' sake,
for theirs is the kingdom of heaven."

Perceiving, perhaps, that his followers will have difficulty absorbing this statement, Jesus immediately amplifies his meaning in the next verses: "'Blessed are you when people revile you and persecute you and utter all kinds of evil against you falsely on my account. Rejoice and be glad, for your reward is great in heaven, for in the same way they persecuted the prophets who were before you'" (Matt. 5:11-12).

The life that perseveres in faithfulness lives both from and for Another.
—Stephen V. Doughty

Of all the beatitudes, surely this is the hardest to take in. Persecution is scarcely our idea of blessedness. To be jeered, harassed, or falsely accused are not exactly happy experiences. Jesus almost appears to have saved the worst for last. Yet from the standpoint of faith, digging deeper into the paradox of God's reign in this world can help us uncover blessedness even in the experience of persecution.

Surely it is not accidental that this last beatitude directly follows one concerning peace. Without a deep experiential knowledge of God's peace, we will not have courage, faith, hope, or love sufficient to withstand the test of persecution. Just as the gift of God's peace provides ground for our peacemaking, so its power enables us to stand firm in the face of opposition to the gospel. Peace grounds us, brings certainty to our faith, and gives us equilibrium when we encounter efforts to destroy the way of peace.

So the blessing pronounced on the work of peace prepares us for

Jesus' final blessing of faithfulness in the face of persecution, to which the previous beatitudes have already introduced us. If we have begun to live the way of blessedness, we already know the experience of opposition. The world around and within us resists the way of God embodied in the beatitudes as a whole. In a world full of itself, full of self-will and disbelief, the way into the joy of the kingdom is not easily entered. Here Jesus reminds us of the cost of discipleship. As the consummate realist, he wants us to be prepared.

Persecution and Testing

What forms of persecution do we face as Christians in our time? This question challenges us. Those of us in a Christianized West are inclined to believe that the age of martyrdom is long past. Our images of persecution still take the shape of Roman amphitheaters and lions. But martyrdom remains a contemporary reality, even in our own country. Martin Luther King Jr. was assassinated because he spoke truth to entrenched powers of racial preference and inequality. Archbishop Oscar Romero was executed by a death squad in the very cathedral he served because he championed the poor and oppressed of El Salvador. In many parts of the world today Christian minorities face harassment, denial of career opportunities, and restricted freedoms. Some even face imprisonment, torture, and death. Of course, people other than Christians also face persecution. The citizens and governments of certain countries routinely abuse ethnic and religious minorities. Other religious traditions have their own understanding of the glories of martyrdom.

Christians understand the reality of persecution by reflecting on Jesus' life and words. To speak God's truth to powers invested in systemic untruth puts us at risk. Human nature has not changed much in the two thousand years since Jesus' crucifixion for alleged sedition against imperial Rome. Yet few of us actually expect to be persecuted for our faith. Our culture has come to consider abundance, control, and comfort as virtually inalienable rights:

Tepid Christianity arouses no one's ire or resistance.
—Mary Lou Redding

We expect that there will be perks to following Christ…that we will at least have stable, happy families, peace of mind, good health care if not good health, and various psychological advantages because of our faith…. For most of us, being a Christian carries no physical, social, or career risk, and we are glad to be able to say that we have never had a sense of being persecuted for our faith.[1]

What, we might wonder, *does this say about the depth of our commitment?* Fifty years ago, Clarence Jordan asked, "Is our light so dim that the tormentor can't see it?"[2] He suggested that the teachings on salt and light that immediately follow the beatitudes serve as Jesus' warning to his disciples: If we lose our power to be salt, the world will simply discard Christianity and trample it underfoot. In becoming weak and "lukewarm" (Rev. 3:15-16), we will succeed in making ourselves irrelevant. Moreover, hiding the light of God's glory is as impossible as trying to hide a city visible on a hill. Since we can't escape the witness of faith, we should let it shine so that others "might see your lovely ways and give the credit to your spiritual Father" (Matt. 5:16).[3]

Enduring comes from knowing a thing inside, not because someone else tells us.
—Sue Monk Kidd

What are our "lovely ways"? What opportunities does God set before us to show our faithful witness, our obedience to divine love in the midst of an unloving, fearful, and greedy world? These questions invite us to consider ways the Spirit moves in us daily to give glory to God. For some, the occasion will come in the mundane routines of family life. In some homes, the unsupported way of Christ in the lone disciple invites sneers, jokes, or dismissal by other family members. Others may experience this kind of treatment in the workplace. Cynicism, prejudice, or commonly accepted unethical practices pervade many work environments. Holding onto integrity as Christian disciples in such places may result in social isolation.

Nor is the church immune from faithlessness. Too many congregations witness more clearly to devilish power struggles than to the godly restraint of humility. We see the evidence in vindictive arguments, personal character attacks, false allegations, and efforts on the part of some to ruin the reputations of others. Often these dynamics swirl around the figure of the pastor, priest, or minister. On a larger scale,

Christians with strong social or political agendas may engage in persecution of other Christians who, in good faith, believe differently. The tactics used are those of the world: accusation, innuendo, power politics, condemnation, and rejection. Persecution within the church occurs more often than we might like to think.

We also persecute ourselves in various ways. Insecurity dominates our inner landscape. We may ridicule our own ideas and accomplishments or undermine ourselves through doubt and self-condemnation. In most middle-class church settings, we find that our persecutors "will, in all probability, not be obvious enemies, but our friends and neighbours, and, not least, ourselves."[4] These relatively mild experiences of persecution pale by historical standards, but the tide of history is already changing. Militant fundamentalists of other faiths often see Westerners, especially Christians, as enemies. We could, once again, know serious persecution.

The key to creative suffering is to find God in the passing moment.

—Ann Callender

Whether in the home, workplace, church, nation, or world, authentic, faithful Christians are arresting. "They confront you with an entirely different way of life, a new way of thinking, a changed set of values, and a higher standard of righteousness."[5] They are hard to ignore. To live the love of Christ and the peace of God truly offers the world more than it is prepared to handle.

Part of the inner dynamic of persecution is the way skittish and unsure people test the reality of God's love. Deeply unsure of ourselves, we put on "spiritual makeup" to appear presentable to God, others, and even ourselves. God's gentle, penetrating truth requires that we give up our public face. If unready to do this, we may become hostile. We may also "act out" like teenagers testing the limits of their parents' love. We seem able only to test love by hurting it. So we sometimes hurt God and those who are like God to see if we are loved for ourselves or for our behavior: "You say you love me for what I really am. All right, then, see if you can love this."[6]

The Happiness of Love's Way

If we truly love, we will know the pain of love tried and wounded. But herein lie the blessing and happiness of the Christlike way. The world's opposition has not frightened the true martyrs (witnesses) of the church away from their faith. Quite the contrary, they have found deep joy in bearing faithful witness to God's truth in their trials. How does this joy come to us? Of what does it consist?

Faithfulness has its own reward, "a sense of satisfying joy in the heart."[7] What we endure for the sake of God's right order does not wound us the way our sin does. The joy of knowing we have acted with integrity before God and in accord with our deepest convictions accompanies our faithfulness. We secure the happiness of a conscience at peace with itself and the world. Beneath the suffering of following Christ resides an inner testimony of gladness, even mirth. We know the gift of a deeper and more abiding life, the joy of goodness and soul-health.

Christians do not seek the happiness of the spiritual life for its own sake. Happiness is not the goal, for it can't be gotten directly any more than humility can be. It comes sneaking into our hearts as we seek the reign of God's holy will. As we mature in spirit, we learn the greater joy in pleasing God than in pleasing ourselves. We discover the greater sweetness in mercy than in revenge, more reality in the unseen than the seen, deeper joy in outgoing love than in self-satisfaction.

The central paradox of the Christian life is that the way of the cross leads through death to greater life than we can imagine. Our earthly joys are so meager compared with what God wants to give us. That joy will be known in its fullness only in the mystery of the life to come. God is forever fashioning a new heaven and earth from all the frayed, damaged threads of our lives. But we can know this joy even now with surprising richness as we give ourselves to God and to others through the love of God.

Sue Monk Kidd, writing of the forced evacuation from her home during Hurricane Floyd, captures a significant quality in the human experience of endurance:

No matter how hard you think your trials are or how much affliction you think they cause you, they will be a source of comfort to you.

—Teresa of Ávila

I grow aware of something unusual happening inside of me. It's as if I am being pared down like a piece of fruit, stripped, peeled, distilled. The events are exfoliating. They shuck me down to some bedrock place that is thick with luminosity and resilience, an enduring inner ground. What comes rising to my lips is the word *God*, and in the next breath, *home*.[8]

This "bedrock place…thick with luminosity and resilience" enables us to withstand life's greatest difficulties, even persecution. This luminous place within is indeed our heart's true home. Here we know our identity as children of God and live out our participation in the kingdom of heaven.

This bedrock place is also the source of the love that "endures all things" (1 Cor. 13:7). Through enduring love we enter with Christ into God's redemptive suffering for the whole creation. What a privilege to join in the self-emptying love of Christ for others. What incomparable joy to play even the tiniest part in God's redeeming grace for a lost and wounded world!

Here is the certainty that upholds us in times of discouragement, trial, and persecution: All the powers of darkness together cannot stand up to God. They are no match for the glory of Love at the heart of the universe. "The light shines in the darkness, and the darkness did not overcome it" (John 1:5). This is our great happiness, our deep blessedness—to be part of the great tide of God's transforming life in this world, sharing in the beauty of God's reign that even now is gathering all things to itself.

Faith comes to the rescue when knowledge fails….It incorporates present, past and future suffering into a vision of ultimate wholeness.

—Ann Callender

DAILY EXERCISES

Read Week Nine, "The Deep Gladness of Suffering Love." Note your thoughts in your journal. As you begin this last week of daily exercises, let your reflections draw from the fullness of your journey through *The Way of Blessedness*. What new vision have you received of the blessed life and the kingdom of God? Where have you sensed God calling you to respond in some specific way? Begin each time of reflection by spending a few minutes to center yourself. Receive God's love and generous goodwill toward all of creation. Invite God to be present with you and draw you into a deepening relationship.

EXERCISE 1   LISTENING TO JESUS

Read Matthew 5:10-12. As you listen to Jesus' blessing, pray for those who are "persecuted for righteousness' sake." When the faithful come to mind, lift them to God and bless them. If no one comes to mind, pray for those you don't know who do indeed share the sufferings of Christ on our behalf.

Try to recall a time when you faced hardship because you were a Christian or because you participated in bearing witness to a value for which Christ stands. Describe the time and your feelings about it now. Or recall a time when you avoided an opportunity to bear witness in a way that might have been disadvantageous. Describe the time and how you feel about it today.

Explore who and what Jesus blesses with this beatitude. Conclude by writing a paraphrase of the beatitude.

In prayer, ask Christ to show you where he wants you to stand with him and for him.

EXERCISE 2   ENDURING THE FIERY FURNACE

Read Daniel 3:8-30. This story of the four in the furnace encourages us, as it encouraged the Israelite exiles in Babylon, to remain true to our faith in the face of opposition. Recall the fiery furnaces you have passed through. How have you experienced God's sustaining presence with you in the furnace?

Reflect now on the fiery furnace that awaits you if you choose to uphold your beliefs and values in a particular situation. If you were to act, where would you (or do you) feel the heat most intensely?

Draw an image of the "fiery furnace" that faithfulness to God could draw you into. Inside it, write the names of several "companions" who stand with you in that challenge. In prayer, enter the scene of your fiery furnace and practice an awareness of God's presence there with you and your companions. What is God calling and giving you courage to do? Record your thoughts and experience.

EXERCISE 3   FIXING YOUR GAZE ON CHRIST

Read Acts 6:8-15; 7:51-60. Stephen, like the apostles and other followers of Jesus, experienced violent opposition to the intrusion of the gospel truth into the status quo. Yet he endured his dying with the same "grace and power" (6:8) that filled his living. What gave Stephen the grace and power to persevere to the end in his witness? Reread the story and search for the source of Stephen's Christlike composure.

Where do you feel called to offer a witness to Christ or to attempt a peacemaking that might be met with hostility? Join Stephen who "gazed into heaven" and beheld the glory of Christ crucified for righteousness' sake. What form and pattern of prayer gives you the necessary strength to persevere?

EXERCISE 4   SUFFERING IN ACCORDANCE WITH GOD'S WILL

Read 1 Peter 4:12-19. Peter calls us to "rejoice," not in suffering for its own sake but "insofar as you are sharing Christ's sufferings" in God's will. In your journal, list some of the sufferings (diminishments, troubles, sacrifices, hardships) you undergo. Reflect on whether you suffer for yourself or with Christ "in accordance with God's will" and call. What difference do you discern?

Identify the places where Christ may be calling you to participate more fully in his life of service and suffering in pursuit of God's will. Now list three to five spiritual practices or other support that you would need to have in place before you can see yourself having the spiritual strength to participate gladly.

In prayer, entrust yourself to a faithful Creator, while continuing to do good.

EXERCISE 5   PERSEVERING IN GRACE

Read Hebrews 12:1-11. What persons, historical or contemporary, make up your "cloud of witnesses"? Draw an image of a cloud, the cloud of divine presence that surrounds your life in Christ. Write into the cloud names of those whose remembrance and companionship encourage, teach, guide, and inspire you.

Beneath your cloud draw a path. At the end of the path, the goal line, write "the joy that is set before us." Meditate on the joy for which Jesus endured the cross. Describe in your own words the vision of the joy for which you would persevere.

At the beginning of the path, write "lay aside." Ponder what Jesus gave up for "the joy…before him." Jot down what you need to lay aside in order to run the race in freedom and joy. What weight and sin cling to you closely?

Under the path, write "running with perseverance." Name the spiritual practices and supports that you plan to put in place for your continued journey on the way of blessedness.

Pray for what you need in order to persevere in grace.

Remember to review the insights recorded in your notebook or journal for the week in preparation for the group meeting.

An Annotated Resource List from Upper Room Ministries

*T*he following books relate to and expand on the subject matter of the Beatitudes. As you read and share with your small group, you may find some material that particularly challenges or helps you. If you wish to pursue individual reading on your own or if your small group wishes to follow up with additional resources, this list may be useful. The Upper Room has published all of the books listed; the number in parentheses is the product number to give when ordering. To order or for assistance, call toll-free 1-800-972-0433.

EMBRACING OUR SPIRITUAL POVERTY
Dimensions of Prayer: Cultivating a Relationship with God (0-8358-0971-4) by Douglas V. Steere, Foreword by E. Glenn Hinson
In a rereleased version of his classic book, Steere answers common questions and concerns about prayer. This easy-to-read book offers new pray-ers an engaging introduction to prayer while providing valuable wisdom for mature Christians.

Gathered in the Word: Praying the Scripture in Small Groups (0-8358-0806-8) by Norvene Vest
For those thirsting for God, Vest describes *lectio divina*, an age-old form of devotional reading that is intended specifically for spiritual nourishment.

Total Devotion to God: Selected Writings of William Law (0-8358-0901-3), compiled and introduced by Keith Beasley-Topliffe

In selections from his book *A Serious Call to a Devout and Holy Life*, William Law writes that the truly devout must live their lives in utter accordance with the will of God.

The Workbook on Virtues and the Fruit of the Spirit (0-8358-0854-8) by Maxie Dunnam and Kimberly Dunnam Reisman
By looking at the seven cardinal virtues and the fruit of the spirit, this study leads us to be persons we were created to be.

TEARS AS ANGUISH, TEARS AS GIFT
Abiding Hope: Encouragement in the Shadow of Death (0-8358-0959-5) by Ann Hagmann
Drawing its inspiration from the psalms, this book of encouragement for those in the valley of the shadow of death, whether in illness or as a caregiver, contains real-life illustrations that tell of persons who seek meaning and peace in the transition from this life to eternal life.

Breaking and Mending: Divorce and God's Grace (0-8358-0855-6) by Mary Lou Redding
Redding's book weaves her personal story with those from scripture to help other Christians who are facing divorce find God's grace in the midst of pain. *Breaking and Mending* looks at the spiritual issues of divorce rather than the sociological ones and allows the scriptures to illuminate and heal those in this difficult transition.

Release: Healing from Wounds of Family, Church, and Community (0-8358-0775-4) by Flora Slosson Wuellner
In her sensitive and compassionate book, Wuellner addresses the emotional burdens and psychic wounds we inherit from our communities and provides guided meditations and healing prayers for whole communities.

When the World Breaks Your Heart: Spiritual Ways of Living with Tragedy (0-8358-0842-4) by Gregory S. Clapper

In this helpful book, Clapper draws on his experience of ministering to those around the crash of United Airlines Flight 232 in Sioux City, Iowa. Clapper's book offers hope for living with tragedies that inevitably come to us all and helps us see God's presence in the midst of these tragedies.

THE POWER OF A CLEAR AND GENTLE HEART

Discovering Community: A Meditation on Community in Christ (0-8358-0870-X) by Stephen V. Doughty

Doughty looks at what it means to be a part of the community of Christ through a number of lenses, focusing on the diverse ways and places in which Christian disciples grow. His book can lead to a renewed sense of personal calling and a revitalized commitment to the mission and ministry of the church.

The Hunger of the Heart: A Workbook (0-8358-0738-X) by Ron Del-Bene with Mary and Herb Montgomery

Designed for individuals or small groups, the six-session workbook includes daily exercises, instructions, and excerpts from *The Hunger of the Heart*.

A Wakeful Faith: Spiritual Practice in the Real World (0-8358-0912-9) by J. Marshall Jenkins

Jenkins writes that it is when we become consciously aware of God's activity in the details of the day that we can transform and find purpose in our lives. Filled with humor and grounded in scripture, *A Wakeful Faith* calls us to a refreshed sense of God's presence, which may lead to spiritual well-being in all dimensions of life.

The Workbook on Keeping Company with the Saints (0-8358-0925-0) by Maxie Dunnam

Draw from the rich well of historic spiritual writing as Maxie Dunnam guides you through the lives and teachings of William Law, Julian of Norwich, Brother Lawrence, and Teresa of Ávila. Discover what

these pioneers of faith teach about being more attuned to God's presence in our lives.

A Satisfying Hunger and Thirst
Reading with Deeper Eyes: The Love of Literature and the Life of Faith (0-8358-0847-5) by William H. Willimon
Good literature allows a reader to glimpse the world through another's eyes and thereby to see in fresh ways God's work in the world. By retelling and interpreting ten classic works of literature, Willimon opens readers to God's revelation through these writings and provides questions to help us examine our own relationship with God.

The Soul's Delight: Selected Writings of Evelyn Underhill (0-8358-0837-8), compiled and introduced by Keith Beasley-Topliffe
This twentieth-century British writer and retreat leader is widely known for her compelling exploration of the spiritual life and her simple but challenging advice on opening oneself to God and living a life of faithfulness.

Spiritual Preparation for Christian Leadership (0-8358-0888-2) by E. Glenn Hinson
Hinson presents a vision of "living saints," the model of spiritual leadership for the church, as people who have experienced God's grace in their lives and are willing to yield themselves to God. Such a vision creates a new understanding of the ways in which the church can be transformed.

Embracing the Wisdom of Tenderness
As If the Heart Mattered: A Wesleyan Spirituality (0-8358-0820-3) by Gregory S. Clapper
Clapper unfolds a vision of the Christian journey by addressing the themes of repentance, faith, and holiness. His book reaches beyond the Wesleyan tradition to speak to the essentials of spiritual life.

Companions in Christ: The Way of Forgiveness (Participant's Book) (0-8358-0980-3) by Marjorie Thompson
Companions in Christ: The Way of Forgiveness (Leader's Guide) (0-8358-0981-1) by Stephen D. Bryant and Marjorie Thompson
The Way of Forgiveness uses scripture meditation and other spiritual practices to guide us through an eight-week exploration of the forgiven and forgiving life. Always keeping God's grace and our blessedness before us, we examine shame, guilt and anger before turning to forgiveness and reconciliation.

Forgiveness, The Passionate Journey: Nine Steps of Forgiving through Jesus' Beatitudes (0-8358-0945-5) by Flora Slosson Wuellner
Wuellner explores the Beatitudes for deeper meanings of forgiveness offered there, helping us recognize new ways of relating to one another within the vision of Jesus. In these blessings we discover an open door to new, healed ways of relating to God, to others, to ourselves, and to the communities around us.

RECEIVING THE VISION OF GOD
Seeking a Purer Christian Life: Sayings and Stories of the Desert Mothers and Fathers (0-8358-0902-1), compiled and introduced by Keith Beasley-Topliffe
The stories of these men and women who sought a simple way of living became the foundation of monasticism.

Where the Heart Longs to Go: A New Image for Pastoral Ministry (0-8358-0849-1) by Thad Rutter Jr.
Through Rutter's book, pastors and other church leaders may gain an awareness of their own spiritual hunger and learn imaginative ways to help others grow in their faith journey.

Wrestling with Grace: A Spirituality for the Rough Edges of Life (0-8358-0985-4) by Robert Corin Morris

Robert Morris helps Christians to develop a keen eye for God's presence in the midst of ordinary life with its reactive emotions and relational struggles. He offers the reader practical ways to let fear, frustration, busyness, and other spiritual blocks become doorways into grace.

Yours Are the Hands of Christ: The Practice of Faith (0-8358-0867-X) by James C. Howell
Christians long to make a difference in the world in faithful response to the call of discipleship. *Yours Are the Hands of Christ* helps us find ways to apply our faith in daily life. Written in a lively, personal style, this book takes a fresh look at familiar moments in the life of Jesus and also draws on the lives of saints through history who are great examples to us of being the hands of Christ today.

MAKING PEACE, AN OFFERING OF LOVE
Climbing the Sycamore Tree: A Study on Choice and Simplicity (0-8358-0946-3) by Ann Hagmann
Climbing the Sycamore Tree examines what it means to be Christ-like in the midst of a materialistic culture. This six-week study for individuals or groups helps readers face everyday choices on the basis of a lifestyle in harmony with Christian beliefs.

Walking Humbly with God: Selected Writings of John Woolman (0-8358-0900-5), compiled and introduced by Keith Beasley-Topliffe
A devout Quaker, Woolman lived simply and traveled throughout the American colonies in the mid-1700s, urging others to stand with him against slavery.

THE DEEP GLADNESS OF SUFFERING LOVE
The Cost of Living: A Personal Journey into John's Gospel (0-8358-0960-9) by Margaret Cundiff
Margaret Cundiff offers a study of John 11–21. This is an opportunity for people caught up in contemporary problems to walk the road

with Jesus through death to life. Cundiff blends illustrations from contemporary ministry with insights into the accounts of Jesus' ministry in the Gospel of John.

Servants, Misfits, and Martyrs: Saints and their Stories (0-8358-0906-4) by James C. Howell
Howell opens a window into the lives of saints whose faith, hope, and action will inspire and encourage readers. These engaging vignettes describe ordinary people who offered themselves fully to God.

Notes

WEEK 1: EXPLORING THE BLESSED LIFE

1. Walter Wink, *Engaging the Powers: Discernment and Resistance in a World of Domination* (Minneapolis, Minn.: Fortress Press, 1992), 111.

2. For most of these insights I am indebted to Walter Wink's chapter titled "God's Domination-Free Order: Jesus and God's Reign" in *Engaging the Powers* (chapter 6).

3. A paraphrase of Clarence Jordan's insight from *Sermon on the Mount* (Valley Forge, Pa.: Judson Press, 1993), 8.

WEEK 2: EMBRACING OUR SPIRITUAL POVERTY

1. Flora Slosson Wuellner, *Forgiveness, the Passionate Journey* (Nashville, Tenn.: Upper Room Books, 2001), 25.

2. Percy C. Ainsworth, *The Blessed Life: Short Addresses on the Beatitudes* (London: Robert Culley, n.d.), 63.

3. Jordan, *Sermon on the Mount*, 10.

4. Ainsworth, *The Blessed Life*, 64.

5. Johannes Baptist Metz, *Poverty of Spirit* (Paramus, N.J.: Paulist Press, 1968), 27.

6. Judy Cannato, "The Poverty of Provisionality," *Weavings* 15, no. 1 (January/February 2000): 12.

WEEK 3: TEARS AS ANGUISH, TEARS AS GIFT

1. Simon Tugwell, *The Beatitudes: Soundings in Christian Traditions* (Springfield, Ill.: Templegate Publishers, 1985), 63.

2. Ibid., 65.

3. Linda J. Vogel and Dwight W. Vogel, *Syncopated Grace: Times and Seasons with God* (Nashville, Tenn.: Upper Room Books, 2002), 67.

WEEK 4: THE POWER OF A CLEAR AND GENTLE HEART

1. A line from "The Seven Deadly Virtues," by Alan Jay Lerner in *Camelot*.

2. A paraphrase of Ainsworth, *The Blessed Life*, 90.

3. Several key ideas in this chapter are developed from insights originally offered by Mary Lou Redding. Of particular note are negative cultural views of meekness in relation to power (page 48), and the interpretation of meekness as human powers placed at God's disposal, including illustrations from Jesus' ministry and of the horse being "gentled" (pages 51–52).

4. Robert C. Morris, "Meek As Moses: Humility, Self-Esteem, and the Service of God," *Weavings* 15, no. 3 (May/June 2000): 39.

5. See Mark Powelson and Ray Riegert, eds., Marcus Borg, consulting ed., *The Lost Gospel Q: The Original Sayings of Jesus* (Berkeley, Calif.: Ulysses Press, 1996), 44.

6. Wink, *Engaging the Powers*, 182.

7. Jordan, *Sermon on the Mount*, 12–13.

8. Morris, "Meek as Moses," 38–9.

9. It is no accident that the marginal people called the Celts developed a rich spirituality embracing the earth and its goodness as signs of God's presence in their midst. Celtic Christians were truly poor, lacking status in the British Isles and often maligned in Christendom. But these people could be said to have inherited th earth, to have enjoyed possession of its beauty and abundance more truly than many Christians who have busily, self-confidently "mastered" and devalued the earth.

WEEK 5: A SATISFYING HUNGER AND THIRST

1. Ainsworth, *The Blessed Life*, 107.

2. Tugwell, *The Beatitudes*, 75.

3. Ibid., 78.

4. Ainsworth, *The Blessed Life*, 107.

5. David Rensberger, "Thirsty for God," *Weavings* 15, no. 4 (July/August 2000): 24.

6. Wendy M. Wright, "I Thirst," *Weavings* 15, no. 4 (July/August 2000): 31.

7. Ainsworth, *The Blessed Life*, 111.

8. Rensberger, "Thirsty for God," 24.

WEEK 6: EMBRACING THE WISDOM OF TENDERNESS

1. Brennan Manning, T*he Wisdom of Tenderness* (San Francisco: HarperSanFrancisco, 2002), 25–26.

2. Ibid., 22.

3. Tugwell, *The Beatitudes*, 87.

4. Robert C. Morris, "God's Wrestling Match with Wrath," *Weavings* 15, no. 5 (September/October 2000): 21–22.

5. Ainsworth, *The Blessed Life*, 127.

6. John McQuiston, *Always We Begin Again: The Benedictine Way of Living* (Harrisburg, Pa.: Morehouse Publishing, 1996), 30–31.

7. See especially James McGinnis's story of being a clown visitor to a seven-year-old boy dying of cancer. "Mercy in Hard Times and Place," *Weavings* 15, no. 5 (September/October 2000): 26–28.

8. Jordan, *Sermon on the Mount*, 17.

9. Ibid., 18.

10. Thomas Merton, *The Sign of Jonas* (Garden City, N.Y.: Doubleday, 1956), 251–52.

Week 7: Receiving the Vision of God

1. Tugwell, *The Beatitudes*, 94.

2. Ibid.

3. Ainsworth, *The Blessed Life*, 135.

4. Tugwell, *The Beatitudes*, 98.

5. Thomas Merton, trans., *The Wisdom of the Desert: Sayings from the Desert Fathers of the Fourth Century* (New York: New Directions Publishing, 1970), 62.

6. Roger Gottlieb, ed., *This Sacred Earth: Nature and the Environment* (New York: Routledge, 1996), 46.

7. Martin Luther, *Luther's Meditations on the Gospels*, trans. by Roland H. Bainton (Philadelphia: The Westminster Press, 1962), 52.

8. Definition of grace offered by Robert Morris to the Pathways-*Weavings* retreat, October 2002, at Scarritt-Bennett Center, Nashville, Tennessee.

9. The contemporary English Blackfriar, Simon Tugwell.

10. Tugwell, *The Beatitudes*, 102.

11. Ibid., 109.

12. Ainsworth, *The Blessed Life*, 140.

13. From "Be Thou My Vision."

Week 8: Making Peace, an Offering of Love

1. W. Paul Jones, "The Heresy of Peace," *Weavings* 13, no. 6 (November/December 1998): 8.

2. Ainsworth, *The Blessed Life*, 148.

3. See full story in Elaine M. Prevallet, "A Kinship Appeal," *Weavings* 13, no. 6 (November/December 1998): 42–43.

4. Ainsworth, *The Blessed Life*, 153.

5. Tugwell, *The Beatitudes*, 121.

Week 9: The Deep Gladness of Suffering Love

1. Mary Lou Redding, unpublished manuscript.

2. Jordan, *Sermon on the Mount*, 26.

3. Ibid., 27.

4. Tugwell, *The Beatitudes*, 133.

5. Jordan, *Sermon on the Mount*, 23.

6. Tugwell, *The Beatitudes*, 131.

7. Ainsworth, *The Blessed Life*, 166.

8. Sue Monk Kidd, "The Secret of Winter Foliage," *Weavings* 15, no. 6 (November/December 2000): 19.

Sources and Authors
of Marginal Quotations

INTRODUCTION

Simon Tugwell, *The Beatitudes: Soundings in Christian Traditions* (Springfield, Ill.: Templegate Publishers, 1985), 79.

WEEK 1: EXPLORING THE BLESSED LIFE

Tugwell, *The Beatitudes*, 74.

Marcus J. Borg, *Meeting Jesus Again for the First Time* (San Francisco: HarperSanFrancisco, 1995), 31.

WEEK 2: EMBRACING OUR SPIRITUAL POVERTY

Evelyn Underhill, "Fruits of the Spirit," letter for Lent, 1941, cited in *The Soul's Delight: Selected Writings of Evelyn Underhill*, ed. Keith Beasley-Topliffe (Nashville, Tenn.: Upper Room Books, 1998), 42.

Johannes Baptist Metz, *Poverty of Spirit* (Paramus, N.J.: Paulist Press, 1968), 27.

Ibid., 47.

Ed Farrell, *Free to Be Nothing* (Collegeville, Minn.: The Liturgical Press, 1989), 116.

WEEK 3: TEARS AS ANGUISH, TEARS AS GIFT

Gregory of Nyssa, *De Beatitudine*, III, PG 44, 1224C, quoted in George Maloney, S.J., *Inward Stillness* (Denville, N.J.: Dimension Books, 1976), 113.

Walter Wangerin, *Mourning into Dancing* (Grand Rapids, Mich.: Zondervan Publishing House, 1992), 232.

Tugwell, *The Beatitudes*, 65.

Deborah Smith Douglas, "Wounded and Healed," *Weavings* 15, no. 2 (March/April 2000): 23.

WEEK 4: THE POWER OF A CLEAR AND GENTLE HEART

Percy C. Ainsworth, *The Blessed Life: Short Addresses on the Beatitudes* (London: Robert Culley, n.d.), 92-93.

John S. Mogabgab, "Editor's Introduction," *Weavings* 15, no. 3 (May/June 2000): 3.

Hannah Whitall Smith, *The Christian's Secret of a Happy Life* (New York: Ballantine, 1986), 22–23.

Tugwell, *The Beatitudes*, 32.

Ainsworth, *The Blessed Life*, 96.

Ben Campbell Johnson, *Calming the Restless Spirit: A Journey toward God* (Nashville, Tenn.: Upper Room Books, 1997), 130.

WEEK 5: A SATISFYING HUNGER AND THIRST

Teresa of Ávila, *The Way of Perfection*, ed. Henry L. Carrigan (Brewster, Mass.: Paraclete Press, 2000), 101.

Wendy M. Wright, *The Rising: Living the Mysteries of Lent, Easter, and Pentecost* (Nashville, Tenn.: Upper Room Books, 1994), 87.

Ronald S. James, "Looking at Power," *Weavings* 14, no. 3 (May/June 1999): 9.

David Rensberger, "Thirsty for God," *Weavings* 15, no. 4 (July/August 2000): 20.

Mogabgab, "Editor's Introduction," 2.

Week 6: Embracing the Wisdom of Tenderness

Tugwell, *The Beatitudes*, 86.

Rodger Nishioka and Judy Kuo, quoted in Dorothy C. Bass and Don C. Richter, eds., *Way to Live: Christian Practices for Teens* (Nashville, Tenn.: Upper Room Books, 2002), 228.

Helen Bruch Pearson, *Mother Roots: The Female Ancestors of Jesus* (Nashville, Tenn.: Upper Room Books, 2002), 146.

Wright, *The Rising*, 40.

Clarence Jordan, *Sermon on the Mount* (Valley Forge, Pa.: Judson Press, 1993), 17.

William Shakespeare, *The Merchant of Venice*, 4.1.180–82.

Week 7: Receiving the Vision of God

Hagmann, *Climbing the Sycamore Tree*, 71.

Ainsworth, *The Blessed Life*, 137.

Carlo Carretto, *The Desert in the City* (New York: Crossroad, 1982), 33.

Tugwell, *The Beatitudes*, 101.

Ainsworth, *The Blessed Life*, 135.

Jordan, *Sermon on the Mount*, 19.

Week 8: Making Peace, an Offering of Love

Tugwell, *The Beatitudes*, 111.

Jordan, *Sermon on the Mount*, 20.

Ainsworth, *The Blessed Life*, 150.

Hildegard of Bingen, *Hildegard von Bingen's Mystical Visions: Translated from Scivias* (Sante Fe: Bear & Co., 1995), 255.

Angela of Foligno, *Angela of Foligno: Complete Works*, trans. Paul Lachance (Mahwah, N.J.: Paulist Press, 1993), 289–90.

Week 9: The Deep Gladness of Suffering Love

Stephen V. Doughty, "Something Better," *Weavings* 15, no. 6 (November/December 2000): 14.

Mary Lou Redding, unpublished manuscript.

Sue Monk Kidd, "The Secret of Winter Foliage," *Weavings* 15, no. 6 (November/December 2000): 23.

Ann Callender, *Pathways through Pain: Women's Journeys* (Cleveland, Oh.: Pilgrim Press, 1999), 100.

Teresa of Ávila, *The Way of Perfection*, 113.

Ann Callender, *Pathways through Pain*, 132.

COMPANION SONG
Piano Accompaniment Score

Lyrics by Marjorie Thompson

Music by Dean McIntyre

Optional cut for short version: omit measures 19-34.

About the Authors

Marjorie J. Thompson is perhaps best known as the author of *Soul Feast*, a book on Christian spiritual practice that is widely used both in congregations and seminaries. She has also written a book on the spiritual nurture of children in the home entitled *Family: The Forming Center* (Upper Room Books, 1996).

In 1996 Marjorie became Director of the Pathways Center for Spiritual Leadership, a program position with Upper Room Ministries. She played a central role in the development of the core resource, *Companions in Christ*, and continues as Spiritual Director to the program.

Marjorie is an ordained minister in the Presbyterian Church, USA. She studied Christian Spirituality with Henri Nouwen at Yale Divinity School as a Research Fellow, subsequently developing a ministry of retreat leadership, spiritual direction, teaching, and writing. Before accepting the position with Upper Room Ministries, Marjorie served as adjunct faculty for several seminaries and taught for Stillpoint (programs in spiritual direction and contemplative prayer) in Nashville.

Stephen D. Bryant is editor and publisher of Upper Room Ministries. His vision of small groups as important settings for spiritual formation and his experience in the contemplative life as well as local churches provided the inspiration for the Companions in Christ series. Stephen was instrumental in shaping the foundational twenty-eight-week *Companions* resource and continues to shape and cowrite the subsequent resources in the series.

Before his election as editor and publisher, Stephen, an ordained minister in The United Methodist Church, served as the Director of Spiritual Formation for The Upper Room and as the International Director of The Walk to Emmaus and Chrysalis movements. He holds a certificate in Theology of Christian Spirituality from Lehb Shomea House of Prayer in Sarita, Texas—a center for contemplative prayer and spiritual theology related to Oblate School of Theology in San Antonio, Texas. He studied with the Shalem Institute of Spiritual Formation.